Drip By Drip
Day By Day

Finding Purpose
Through The Pain

Steven Russell

DRIP BY DRIP DAY BY DAY: FINDING PURPOSE THROUGH THE PAIN
Authored by Steven Russell
© Steven Russell, 2025

ISBN: 978-1-0685905-7-3
Edited by Marcia M Publishing House Editorial Team
Cover design, printing & binding: Marcia M Publishing House Ltd.
Published by Marcia M Spence of Marcia M Publishing House Ltd.
On behalf of Steven Russell, In West Bromwich, West Midlands the UNITED KINGDOM B71.
All rights reserved 2025 Steven Russell

All photographs are the property of Steven Russell who holds the right to publish this work. All videos are the property of Steven Russell.

Steven Russell asserts the moral right to be identified as the author of this work. The opinions expressed in this published work are those of the author and do not reflect the opinions of Marcia M Publishing House Team.

This book is a memoir, written from Steven Russell's memories and care records, full names and descriptions of places and people, in some instances have been changed or omitted to protect the privacy of individuals and organisations.

This book is sold subject to the conditions it is not, by way of trade or otherwise, lent, hired out or otherwise circulated in any form of binding or cover other than that in which it is published. No part of this publication may be reproduced, stored in a retrieval system or transmitted in any form or by any means (electronic, mechanical, photocopying, recording or otherwise) without prior written permission from the Author.

A copy of this publication is legally deposited in The British Library.

www.marciampublishing.com

Dedication

To Dave, my unwavering source of strength; to Pat, who gave me my first experience of a mother's love; to Adam, my best friend from school who always had my back; and to Eunice and Neville, my final foster carers who allowed me to truly be myself. Five key people who have impacted me profoundly.

Foreword

by Fatima Whitbread, MBE

In *"Drip by Drip, Day by Day: Finding Purpose Through the Pain,"* Steven Russell invites us on a deeply personal and profoundly universal journey. From a childhood marked by instability and the search for belonging, Steven weaves a narrative of resilience, hope, and the transformative power of human connection.

Prepare to be moved by Steven's unflinching honesty and courageous spirit. He shares his experiences within the care system not as a victim, but as a survivor who has not just navigated the storms but has emerged determined to help others find their own paths to healing and purpose.

Steven invites you into a world few dare to explore with such raw honesty and unwavering hope. *"Drip by Drip, Day by Day: Finding Purpose Through the Pain"* is more than just a memoir; it's a testament to the resilience of the human spirit and a roadmap for anyone seeking light in the darkest of circumstances. It offers hope for anyone who has ever felt lost, alone, or disconnected.

Steven's story, woven with threads of adversity and triumph, speaks directly to the heart. His voice is a light, guiding us to confront our own challenges with courage and find purpose even amidst pain. He doesn't shy away from the difficult truths of his journey; instead, he embraces them, offering us profound insights and a renewed sense of possibility.

The essence of Steven's story mirrors my own journey – being abandoned as a baby and, some would say, left to die, and spending the first fourteen years of my life in care. Sport was my saviour, and through sport, I found the love of the Whitbreads and achieved success not only as a sports person but in life. It is because of these experiences that I have founded Fatima's UK Campaign – a charity focusing on bringing fundamental change to the care system so that children like Steven and I have a very different experience.

This story will resonate with care leavers, social workers, foster parents, and anyone committed to making a difference in the lives of vulnerable children. It offers insights, inspiration, and a powerful reminder that every connection matters, every act of empathy can create ripples of change, and every individual has the power to transform their pain into purpose.

This book is an invitation to reflect, to empathize, and to discover the extraordinary strength that lies within each of us. Prepare to be inspired, challenged, and ultimately uplifted by the power of Steven's words.

His story is a testament to the idea that even in the face of adversity, we can find strength in the smallest acts of kindness, in unwavering support, and in the quiet determination to keep moving forward to carve out a brighter future, one drip at a time.

Open these pages and allow Steven to guide you on a journey of healing, purpose, and unwavering belief in the power of the human spirit.

Contents

Preface 1

One: Press Rewind 13

Two: Roots 20

Three: Never Forever 41

Four: Dave 51

Five: Little Steven's voice 66

Six: Removed 74

Seven: Chameleon 80

Eight: A Black and White World 84

Nine: Rejection, The Labels 90

Ten: The Search for Belonging 97

Eleven: I'm Not a Care Leaver 119

Twelve: Torn 131

Thirteen: Melting The Ice 157

Fourteen: Living In My Shadow 172

Fifteen: Purpose 184

Sixteen: To Those Who Are Struggling 186

Seventeen: The Power of One 191

Eighteen: Letters to Steven 201

Nineteen: Dear Steven 211

About the Author 222

Preface

Drip by Drip, Day by Day: Finding Purpose Through the Pain

I have to admit, when I first thought about writing my autobiography, I struggled with what to call it. My initial idea was, *"The Journey of Little Steven"*, a title that reflects the deeply personal nature of this story. But as I sat with the intention behind the book, it became clear that the title needed to be broader, something that reached far beyond my own experiences.

It's true, there was no silver spoon. No stability, no inheritance, no little attachment to caregivers. My purpose doesn't come from life's comforts, and nor should it.

Looking back now, I recognise the unique challenges that little boy faced, trying so hard to find his place in a world that felt indifferent. Moving from one home to another was like pressing the reboot button repeatedly. New places, new faces, new rules. It was a life without continuity, each chapter starting with disjointed introductions and abrupt endings. It felt like living on quicksand, always shifting, never firm. The exhaustion was deeper than just physical; it seeped into my bones, into the core of who I was becoming.

This book is not just my story. It's about all of us who have been shaped by the care system. Those of us who identify as care leavers, (although not a term I use myself) and the professionals who strive daily to support, champion, and advocate for care-experienced people. I wanted a title that would resonate with anyone connected to this world, a phrase that captured the resilience, determination, and quiet strength of the care-experienced community.

For as long as I've worked with young people, my mantra has remained the same: *Drip by drip, day by day.* Recently, I added a new line to it - *We find a way.* People often ask me, "*What does it mean? Where does it come from?*"

The truth is, this phrase has many origins and interpretations, but to truly understand, we must return to where it all began.

The Ice That Turns into Water

Growing up in the care system can feel like being adrift in a sea of uncertainty; lost, abandoned, and rejected. When you're moved from house to house, school to school, and family to family, you lose the thread of who you are. You become a temporary resident in your own life, unsure of what stability or belonging is supposed to look like.

For me, friendships were fleeting, built on borrowed time, collapsing the moment the bags were packed again. Buildings were temporary; tall, lonely structures that felt as hollow as my sense of belonging. Every home carried its own rhythm; some hesitantly warm, and others colder than the silence. I learned early that people's kindness could be fleeting too, that warmth didn't always linger.

That was my reality. I found myself navigating a world that felt distant, lonely, and unbearably cold. I didn't just feel disconnected. I *was* disconnected. I was searching for warmth, begging for connection, yet all I received was disappointment.

I used to wrestle with the reality of growing up in places where I didn't belong. The words "Mum" and "Dad" felt foreign on my tongue. I envied the ease with which my classmates used them, unaware of how precious and alien they felt to a boy like me. In the lead up to Mother's Day and Father's Day, I'd plaster on a smile as my peers glued hearts and glitter to cards destined for parents waiting at home. Their parents weren't just an idea; they were a presence.

Over time, I realised coldness has a way of hardening you. Frozen in place, that cold can transform into ice. And once it does, it's a struggle to break free from its grasp. It's strange now to hear the adults, reflecting on my younger self, describing me as cold and distant. There's an eerie truth to their words. What they didn't see then, but what I've come to learn now, is that no child becomes cold on their own.

Christmases were particularly piercing, the joy of it almost mocking. My classmates would buzz with excitement, counting down to a kind of celebration that didn't seem real in my world. The closest I came to that cheer was hearsay. Holidays were landmarks of absence, reminders of what I didn't have. The ache of that emptiness wasn't loud; it was quiet and insidious.

And so, as an adult, I've thought a lot about how we respond to children who've been wrapped in ice. *What can we do to reach that frozen core? How can we be the ones to help them thaw?*

This is where I developed the foundation of *Drip by drip, day by day*. To support a child with trauma, it isn't enough to simply understand what they've been through. It requires more than training, or knowledge, or repeating buzzwords like *trauma informed*. We need to move beyond mere awareness.

Instead, we must be *trauma responsive*. To be trauma-responsive means taking what we know about trauma and applying it, not just as a theory, but as a guiding principle for how we create policies, environments, and practices that are truly therapeutic for the young people in our care.

It also means interrogating the lens through which we view these children. Over the years, I've seen three types of approaches that adults use when responding to the *ice* in a child's life: apathy, sympathy, and empathy. Each of these approaches has a ripple effect, however only one of them has the power to transform.

Apathy, Sympathy, and Empathy

Apathy has no place in the care sector, but it often sneaks in through the back door when compassion fades. We tell ourselves that the issues are, "not my problem," that the child's pain is, "too much to handle". Terms like, "Hard to Reach" or "change is beyond our grasp", are used. Sometimes, apathy stems from burnout, the relentless cycle of stress and *compassion fatigue* forcing people to shut down.

Sympathy, by contrast, offers small warmth but no real change. Sympathy says, "I'm sorry this happened to you," but keeps its distance. It feels for the child, but it doesn't connect deeply enough to ignite a transformation. It sees the ice but doesn't step into the cold.

Then there's empathy. *Compassionate Empathy* is what I call the glue to connection. It bridges the gap between cold and warmth; it doesn't have all the answers, but it has the courage to sit in uncertainty with the child. Compassionate Empathy says, "I see your pain. I don't have the same story as you, but I know how isolation, anger, and rejection feel and together, we'll find a way forward."

Apathy is cold; sympathy is lukewarm; empathy is warm. And when warmth meets ice, something incredible happens. The ice melts. Not all at once, and not without effort, but *drip by drip, day by day*. And in that slow, patient process, we build trust. We plant the seeds of connection.

A Ripple That Breaks the Waves

Another way to describe *Drip by drip, day by day,* is to think of a single droplet in the ocean. On its own, one droplet appears insignificant. But with time, those droplets form streams, rivers, and oceans. That one droplet achieves something far greater than it could in isolation. It becomes part of a vast, collective force. This is what community, belonging, and family look like for children in care.

Drip by drip, day by day, reminds us that every small act of connection matters. Every moment of warmth, patience, and authenticity builds something larger; a village that raises the child, a home that provides belonging, and an environment that creates purpose.

None of this happens overnight. It's a slow, deliberate process but it's worth every moment and every drip.

Why This Book Exists

In 2022, I trademarked the phrase *Drip by drip, day by day*. Not because chasing trademarks interests me, but because a good friend warned me, "If you don't, someone else will." It turns out they were right, this mantra seems to resonate far and wide. And now, it's become the anchor of this book.

To the young person reading this book, know this, the words within these pages are mine, but the hope they carry belongs to us both. My wish is that, by the final chapter, you'll find a sense of purpose within your own story.

To the social workers, foster carers, kinship carers, residential carers, teachers, and everyone devoted to walking alongside vulnerable children. I salute you. Your work is often invisible, but it changes lives in immeasurable ways, without you, stories like mine wouldn't exist.

And finally, to my care-experienced brothers and sisters, this book is a tribute to you. Our experiences are unique, yet they share a common resilience. We've known pain, but we've also fought for joy, meaning, and belonging. My story is merely one thread in the tapestry of care-experienced lives. Together, we will weave, the tapestry, a legacy of strength and fortitude for the next generation to follow.

A Journey Together

Drip by drip, day by day, is no longer just a mantra. It's the heartbeat of a movement. This book is about uncovering purpose through pain, finding sunshine after the storm, and becoming part of something greater than us.

As you turn the pages of this book, know that I am with you, every step of the way. Today, we begin this story together, a story both personal and universal. And I hope, by the final word, you'll find that same quiet assurance I've come to cherish.

Change happens *drip by drip, day by day* and now, it's time for us to find our way.

Drip By Drip
Day By Day

Finding Purpose
Through The Pain

Steven Russell

One

Press Rewind

As I began working on this book, my writing coach asked me to take my mind back. She asked for the very first memory stored in my mind. It was a strange experience for me as my recollections of my childhood are a blend of stories, papers and files collated by other people. Professionals in the main told me who I was and what my history had been and some even forecasted my future. The memory I found is of when I had a sleep over with my Mummy. I believe I was about four years old but I cannot confirm this, just like many of the facts of my life.

I wake up early in the morning, laying on the sofa in the lounge. My mum and her boyfriend H are still in bed. I roll off the sofa onto the floor, then army crawl into my mother's bedroom. I can hear the sound of them breathing deeply and half snoring as they sleep. I see H's jacket on the floor. Poking out of his jacket pocket is a half-opened packet of blackcurrant hard boiled sweets. I reach in carefully, trying not to make too much noise from the crackling of the packet.

I take one sweet out, then army crawl slowly back into the lounge and onto the sofa where I suck and chew the sweetie.

Moments later, after finishing the sweet, I army crawl back into the bedroom, so I can take another sweet. However, this time, I pause in my tracks as I hear movement in the bed but the sleeping sounds continue. As I look up, I notice H's foot sticking out at the end of the bed. His foot looks huge and long with an orange colour to the bottom of his feet with black dots on them. I decide to poke the black dots. However, his foot only recedes back under the bedsheets. I take another sweet then army crawl back into the living room, where I turn on the TV and watch cartoons.

After sharing this memory, other memories flowed…

My foster mum Pat throws a party for my fifth birthday. All my school friends come.

Nowadays, children at birthday parties are all glued to their iPads and mobile phones; but back in my day, even with all the chaos of my childhood, I'm grateful that all the kids were present to sing happy birthday to me. *Mummy comes, with a massive toy clown. It's so big; it's taller than me.*

I vividly remember chewing the clown's red hair. It had a very distinctive taste. It wasn't very nice, but I still found myself continuing to chew it. Looking back, I can only imagine it was a sensory need.

I remember the embarrassment of wetting the bed and the different responses of my caregivers.

What follows are the bare facts of my early infancy; I hardly have any more detail of this period. This is information I have gathered over time about my early life.

I was born on 30th of July 1985 at Marston Green Maternity Hospital. My mummy, from an Irish background was 20 years old and my father 33 had emigrated from Barbados as a teenager.

Believe it or not, my mummy also grew up in care. She would often tell me stories about how she and her sisters had to earn stars by doing chores and behaving well to get visits with their parents. She describes her childhood as turbulent, which, in part, led to her being placed into care.

There's more to the story. My dad was already around when my mum and her sisters were growing up in care, and he built a bond with one of her older sisters. This relationship, which could often be volatile, eventually turned into a marriage and three children were born from it: Trevor, David, and John. My half-brothers and my first cousins. It's also worth noting that my dad had a daughter from an earlier relationship, my half-sister, Trevina.

What I now know is that my dad spent time in Winson Green Prison in 1983 and 1984, serving time for attacking my mummy's sister, his then-wife, with a knife. When he was released, he reconnected with my mummy, and in the summer of 1984, their relationship began. By July of the next year, I was born.

My mummy always told me my dad loved her, and he loved me too. But from everything I've heard and read, their love story was far from simple. They lived at Cleveland Tower in Birmingham, and my dad drove a bright yellow Ford Cortina. He worked in a warehouse and had a talent for making things with his hands. But there was a darker side, especially after he'd been drinking. My mummy admitted that his drinking would often lead to violence and destructive behaviour.

One story she shared always stuck with me. My dad smoked Hamlet cigars and, one evening at a restaurant, he asked her to fetch them. But she misheard, thinking he'd said, "omelette." When she came back and explained it was going to take another 20 minutes to cook, he grew angry and aggressive. She laughed when she recounted the story to me years later, but it was clear it wasn't something she found funny at the time.

Looking back, reading through my care records and piecing together what family have said, it doesn't feel like my dad carried much love for my mummy. It was clear she was in an abusive relationship, trapped in the often-suffocating cycle that domestic violence creates. Still, she spoke of loving him, almost as if saying it might help rewrite their story.

On November 16th, 1985, my dad was killed. It happened when he drove his yellow Ford Cortina straight into someone's living room. The circumstances of his death remain a mystery. The pathologist found barely any alcohol in his system; it wasn't enough to impair his driving. The roads were clear of ice or debris, and he wasn't speeding, driving at around 40 to 50 miles an hour. But two weeks before his death, he had been involved in a pub brawl where someone struck him over the head with a cue stick. Blood had been coming out of his ear, and, according to a friend named Andre, my dad had complained about feeling dizzy and tired in the days that followed. The pathologist concluded it was likely a brain haemorrhage caused by his injury during the fight that led him to lose control of the car.

I was only four months old when he passed away. Two months later, at six months, I was taken into care. Those last few months of 1985 and the start of 1986 would have been unimaginably difficult for my mum. Out of respect for her, there are aspects of her life I've chosen not to include here. But what I can share is that she was fighting battles that left her unable to meet my most basic needs. And so, my life in care began.

My first home was with my Mummy and aunty Sadie at aunty Sadie's house in Bordesley Green Birmingham. The first time I was taken into care was on 24th February 1986. I stayed with foster parents, Mr and Mrs Beswick for a few days. On 27th February 1986, I was moved to live with Mrs Green. Then on 3rd March I went to live back with Mummy at aunty Sadie's house. A while later, Mummy and I moved to our flat in Bordesley Green. On 29th April 1986, I went to live with some foster families. First, Mrs Grey in Great Barr, then Mrs Cooper in Great Barr and then on 10th July 1986, I was moved to stay with Pat. Pat lived in Streetly Birmingham. I was 11 months old at this time. There were multiple moves, to short term foster homes, throughout my first year of life. I don't know why it was so. I was never told the reason.

Baby Steven

Steven's Mum and Dad

Two

Roots

Pat was the first person who ever showed me what a mother could be. I can't remember my experiences with Mummy up to six months of age, but what I can remember is living with Pat between the ages of 11 months and seven years. Pat is a tall British woman who had been fostering since 1983. I believe she was in her late forties when I went to live with her. I went back to visit her, in 2009 and 2023 she's still just as tall. Also, she was surrounded with the familiar scent of fresh linen clothing that I once could smell as a child... The scent of love, warmth and comfort.

Living with Pat was where my first roots were laid, the foundation blocks of my early life built. These were my formative years of growth. My role model of a mother was and will always be Pat. I have many extremely fond memories of being with Pat.

This woman was loving, compassionate, caring, affectionate. Very affectionate, she would always give me cuddles and help me tie my laces. She was very hands on with me. I have pictures of me and Pat on the beach collecting seashells.

Pat was my mother.

As a child, I suffered with nocturnal enuresis, a condition that caused me to wet the bed at nighttime. This was a shameful experience for me, and it was something that persisted until I was 14-15. As you can imagine, having stopovers at my friend's house was quite embarrassing.

I remember walking with Pat on our way to the doctors. A specific clinician that would support this condition. They gave Pat a mesh type of sheet to go underneath my bed sheet. It was hooked up to an alarm system. When the sheet got wet, it would trip the alarm and a high-pitched tone would ring out. I remember clearly coming back home and pat and I putting it on my bed. Pat explained how it worked, "When you have an accident, you will hear the alarm and I will come in and help you get washed and changed." So, the alarm would go off. I would sometimes have a bit of fear, as a child under six, woken by a loud high-pitched tone. But Pat would always come in. She would help me change the sheets and then she'd wash me down, get clean pyjamas on me and tuck me back into bed. That became the routine, so I never worried about bed-wetting afterward because Pat addressed the problem with love, care, and affection. Pat was very supportive towards me when the alarm was triggered. I remember one night; I woke to the sound of the alarm going, signifying I had wet the bed. With my pyjamas soaked in urine, Pat entered my bedroom to soothe me and to nullify any shame I felt. She changed my bed sheets, helped me shower, then settled me back to bed. This was the love I felt from Pat. The warmth of her love.

Pat supported me when I was most vulnerable. One time I was at school, Lindens school infants. I soiled myself; I can't recollect how. Pat saved me by bringing a change of clothes and underwear. I so appreciate the way she cared for me, I was allowed to leave early with Pat. Then on the way back, she would playfully tease me, calling me a silly banana. Pat was fun, she let me do things kids love to do, safe risks like walking on walls.

Pat filled me with safety. Oh man, she filled me up. The fact that I had those first few years with her, gave me that grounding; she gave me that foundation. So, even though the next few years were going to be tough for me and really rocky, she instilled a strong amount of love into me that; I guess, helped me weather the storms of life, moving forward in my childhood.

From a little kid's perspective, Pat's was quite a large house. My bedroom was quite large and I had all my toys in my room. Pat made sure that I always had a variety of toys to play with. The garden was like a child's paradise, it was huge with a climbing frame, swing and a nice big swimming pool.

We had a dog called Toby as well.

That's when swimming pools used to be swimming pools!

Drip By Drip Day By Day

I played a lot of football by myself. I vividly recall being six years old, playing football in the garden. It was a hot, sunny day. The two goalposts were large cooking pots, and I stood there, kicking the ball towards an imaginary goalkeeper that I tried to visualise. I wanted the challenge, someone there to block it, to make me work for it. But no matter how hard I imagined a goalie, that goal was always wide open. I wanted a friend, a brother, a sister, anyone, someone to share those moments with. Yet I learned early on that life doesn't always give you what you want.

Home-cooked meals were regularly prepared by Pat, who consistently engaged in baking cakes and cooking. The aroma of freshly baked cakes often filled the house, while the sizzle of ingredients in the pan created a comforting soundtrack. The sight of golden-brown crusts and vibrant vegetables added to the warm, inviting atmosphere of Pat's kitchen.

I loved when the video man came round with his van filled with VHS cassettes. I would always run out to him with Pat. There were VHS videos stacked up in the back of his van loads of them and Pat would rent a few of them each time. Back then we didn't have satellite or cable television. The best thing was, Pat always allowed me to pick one from the children's section. I loved watching Disney movies like *Fantasia, Never-Ending Story, The Goonies, and Snow White.* I would watch them over and over again.

I went to Lindens Primary School in Streetly, which was an affluent area of Birmingham back then and just a five-minute walk from the house. I lived with Pat and her daughter, Kate. Kate is about 10 years older than me. Kate was always playful and I always felt like she was my big sister. Kate would also help out when it came to bath time and settling me down for bed with bedtime stories.

While living at Pat's, my mummy could come and see me on my birthday and other special occasions. When my mummy used to come over to see me, I used to get a bit upset because I didn't want to be around her. I said things like, "You're not my mummy, go away." Pat was in between a rock and a hard place. I know she wanted me to develop a relationship with my mummy but also, she could see that these visits would upset me. I don't have many fond memories of Mummy's visits.

Pat was an amazing mother to me, a mother who made birthdays special, I would have celebrated my very first birthday at Pat's. That would be nine birthdays celebrated with Pat in total. As I grew older, my school friends would be invited over.

When Pat baked my birthday cake, the whole house would smell like vanilla and sweet goodness. She loved baking. We had all kinds of sandwiches and big chunks of cake instead of tiny slices.

I didn't want Mummy to come on my birthdays mainly because I didn't feel like I knew her. My Mummy was quite direct, she'd keep saying, "I'm your mother, I'm your mum!"

Mummy was always trying to clean me up, wiping my face, my clothes and checking my ears. I was living with Pat and felt a loyalty to Pat you see. I suppose I was so happy with Pat, my mum, that I didn't want a reminder that she wasn't.

Photographs of Mummy remind me of how radiant she looked, a young woman with luminous, smooth skin and striking features that seemed to glow. The gentle waves of her red hair framing her face in a way that accentuated her expressive eyes.

Pat's house was fun we had loads of outdoor play equipment and apparatus. That's when kids use to be kids. I remember these flatpack cars that we had to build, and I would make the sounds of a car using my imagination as if I were the driver. I have fond memories of zooming around Pat's living room in my imaginary car, the vibrant colours of the room blurring as my imagination took over.

Pat would take me to school with the other kids that I lived with as well.

Pat didn't drive. Me and Pat would walk. Pat's a walker. Sometimes I would have to walk carrying bags back from the shops. We walked everywhere; Pat has lived a healthy life. We would only catch a bus if we were travelling a long distance.

One word that really comes to me when I think of Pat is, *available.* Yeah, she was available. Pat was available for me, no matter my emotion, no matter my behaviour. I see Pat as a power of one. She was just there, if I fell down, she was there. If I needed to be told off or I did something wrong, she would tell me. She would always coat it with a comforting hug rather than punitive punishment. This was the loving warmth I felt from Pat.

Christmas celebrations were magical. Pat ensured that all the decorations were carefully arranged, creating a festive atmosphere with Christmas music such as *I Wish It Could Be Christmas Every Day* and *Jingle Bells.*

The living room was adorned with twinkling fairy lights and beautifully decorated garlands draped over the mantelpiece. A magnificent Christmas tree stood in the corner, glistening with ornaments, tinsel, and a shining star on top.

Pat's attention to detail was evident in every aspect of the celebration. Candles flickered softly on the windowsills, casting a warm glow across the room.

The cheerful sounds of classic holiday tunes playing in the background, setting the mood for a day of joy and togetherness. The combination of thoughtful decorations, delicious treats, and joyful music made Christmas at Pat's truly magical and memorable.

Drip By Drip Day By Day

Steven Russell

THIS IS THE CAR WE MADE WITH THE PLAY PANELS I HAD FOR CHRISTMAS.

Drip By Drip Day By Day

I remember our house fully decorated with ceiling ornaments, a tree, tinsel everywhere, and beads. I loved decorating the tree, playing with the Christmas tassel beads, and helping Pat. The joy of hanging each shimmering ornament and stringing the twinkling lights filled our home with warmth and excitement. On Christmas mornings, Pat always had sacks of presents ready for us, each one wrapped with care and tied with a bow. The anticipation as we opened each gift, the laughter, and the shared happiness made those moments unforgettable. Pat's thoughtfulness and the festive atmosphere she created are memories I will cherish forever.

Many children stayed with us for short-term care, often only weeks or months. There were plenty of them, sometimes different children each week, and occasionally babies. Rarely were there children my age; most were younger.

One magical Christmas Eve at Pat's, I thought I saw Father Christmas. Though I knew it was likely a dream, when I woke up, I couldn't shake the feeling of wonder. I eagerly looked out the frosty window and, to my astonishment, I saw him, a glimpse of red and white against the night sky.

Pat would always tell us to go to sleep and let the magic of Christmas unfold. She would read us heartwarming stories, her voice gentle, yet filled with excitement, as she painted vivid pictures of Santa's journey around the world. We left a mince pie for Santa and a glass of milk beside it, along with a bright orange carrot for Rudolf. The anticipation was palpable; we could almost hear the sleigh bells ringing in the distance as we finally drifted off to sleep, clutching our dreams of a magical Christmas morning.

I genuinely believed in Santa because I thought I saw him flying in the sky on his sleigh. For some unknown reason, even to this day, I still have the memory of seeing Santa go past. Somehow, I felt he had seen me. I was looking out of the window, and it was a full moon. I just remember seeing Santa with the reindeers going past the moon.

I recall jumping back into bed and putting the cover over my head. I was obviously dreaming, because we all know that Santa doesn't exist.

As a child, I often drew pictures of soldiers in uniform with guns, but I still don't understand why. I remember sitting and drawing the meticulously detailed uniforms. The guns were always prominent, almost too large for their hands, and I would colour them with a heavy hand, pressing the crayon deep into the paper. Now, I wonder what inspired that fascination. Was it the movies I watched, the stories I heard, or something deeper within my young mind trying to express itself?

I had a blast taking bubble baths. The tub was filled with tons of bubbles, and I got to play with all sorts of toys like action figures, McDonald's toys, soldiers, and even toy cars. I'd create little underwater adventures with them, imagining epic battles and races. It was a real highlight of my day! I used to make my toys dive into the bath bubbles, leaving a hole. Other toys would follow through that same hole as if chasing the first toy. I clearly remember this rule I made.

I used to enjoy emptying the garden shed, taking everything out onto the lawn, tidying up, and putting it back. I remember sweeping out the cobwebs with a broom.

I had warm, happy times at Pat's and enjoyed being home.

I loved entertaining Pat and the family. Once, I played with the garden's boxing ball, letting it hit my face to make everyone laugh. Creating joyful moments for others filled me with joy.

Roots uplifted

My social worker said they were finding my Forever family and that Pat's house was temporary. At that time,

it was never explained to me that race was the fundamental reason I had to leave my mother Pat and everything familiar, including family, school, friends, and community. My social worker came to take a picture of me in the garden for the fostering and adoption newspaper. This was where potential carers could view children available for fostering or adoption. She carefully arranged the setting to capture a warm and inviting atmosphere, hoping it would resonate with those considering bringing a child into their home. The photo session aimed to portray the sense of hope and opportunity waiting for both the children and the future carers. I was *advertised* in the Guardian Newspaper to attract my Forever Family, the idea of a Forever Family is sold to the child in care, "You're going to have a family who will love you and look after you forever." Social workers often framed the adoption or long-term placement in positive, reassuring terms. The word "forever" was deliberately used to contrast temporary foster care arrangements.

Three

Never Forever

I was seven years of age when I was moved to live with my forever family. The family responded to the advert in the Guardian. I was taken from Pat's care and moved in with them. The move took place in early July 1992 just before my 8th birthday. I clearly remember my sense of excitement at having an older brother and sisters, I would be sharing a room with my older brother on bunk beds. My social worker totally noticed that my new siblings looked a lot like me, which should have made fitting into my new family way easier. The dad was tall with dreadlocks and was a bit darker skinned than me and my new *mum* was white; my siblings were the same colour as me. I had a brand-new bike when I arrived, and the area looked posh to me.

Here's a paradox: my new mum was named **Pat**, just like my original mum. I found it difficult to call her "mum," especially since I had never used that term for my biological mother. Yet, she insisted that I should address her as "mum" because I was living under her roof. So, I ended up doing it begrudgingly. Every time I said it, it never felt right. I was calling her mum for her needs and not for mine.

The nocturnal enuresis remained, and while my new *mum* seemed supportive in the early part of my stay, she was not so compassionate towards the end; she ridiculed me and shamed me in front of my foster siblings.

"This is disgusting. You shouldn't be doing this at your age. It's laziness. Why can't you just go to the toilet like a normal child?"

It got to where I was fearful of the repercussions of her finding out I had wet the bed. So, I decided, it would be easier to hide the wet sheets and pyjamas behind the wardrobe than admit to the accident. Then one-day, she came into the room as I lay on the top bunk of my bed.

"What's that smell?" she said, and she opened the windows and emptied the drawers, slamming drawers as she was mumbling to herself in disappointment. Then she moved the wardrobe and pulled out my foul-smelling sheets and pyjamas, which must have been there for weeks. *Mum* pulled me out of my bed aggressively and told me I was disgusting and that I needed to bathe.

Bath times with this *mum* were nothing like my early experiences. There was an occasion when I was drying myself after a bath and she told me to hug her. I didn't have any clothes on and I refused, she became angry, sending me to my room. The slow insidious process of showing me I didn't belong had begun.

Each morning on the way to school, we would stop off at the local shop. With a sinking heart, I watched as my foster mum bought her daughters a delicious *Panda Pop* and a tempting chocolate bar, but I was left empty-handed for being deemed too naughty and cheeky. It felt so unfair and hurtful.

It wasn't long before my arms became covered in bruises from my foster *mum* hitting me. She would smack me and hit me with the wooden spoon or a hanger. I spent significant amounts of time in my bed during the final period with the family. It felt safer in bed. I even planned to run away with my friend Ashton from school. In geography class, we studied the local area and planned to run away using a map. I remember the thrill of plotting our escape routes, imagining the freedom and adventure that awaited us beyond the familiar streets. I never followed through, held back by fear. The dream of running away stayed just a dream. I remember lying in my bed, looking at the map and thinking about it.

One day, I spied on my foster sister when she was getting dressed. My foster *mum* caught me and decided to teach me a lesson, a lesson I wouldn't soon forget.

"How would you like it if people seen you with no clothes on?" she quizzed me. "Take your clothes off." She ordered me. I took my clothes off to my Y-fronts and she said, "take those off as well." It was in front of the girls, feeling humiliated at eight years of age, I took my Y-fronts off. *Mum* grabbed me by the arm and put me outside the front of the house, naked. It was broad daylight. Vehicles were passing by. The experience was highly distressing, causing me to cry and urgently knock on the front door in an attempt to re-enter. The exact duration of my time outside is unclear; however, it was certainly an extensive period for an eight-year-old child to endure such embarrassment and shame.

One night, my foster sisters asked if I wanted to have a sleepover in their bedroom. We had all the quilts on the floor with sweets and pop as we watched TV. When it was time to go to sleep, I was lying between my two sisters. The older sister, who was 15, instructed me to climb on top of her. I recall she had removed her pyjama bottoms and whispered to me to do the same. At this stage, I just remember being very confused about what was happening. I climbed on top of her as instructed. I can't remember much of what happened after that, but I do remember her telling me not to say anything to *mum* as we would both get into big trouble.

I don't have many happy memories from this home, and out of all the families I went to live with, this was clearly the worst I had experienced. My foster *mum* told me one day when we were in the kitchen, *"If your behaviour doesn't improve, you will have to live in a children's home, and do you know what happens in children's homes? You get bullied!"*

On a routine visit, my social worker noticed bruising on my arms. She asked me how I got them, so I just shrugged my shoulders. During the conversation, I had a suspicion someone was listening through the door. I tiptoed over, grabbed the handle, and pulled the door open as fast as I could. As I did, my foster *mum* and two sisters fell through the door!

They tried to pretend they were not eavesdropping, by asking if we wanted a drink. It was evident they were indeed actively listening to the private meeting between me and my social worker. I think my social worker must have looked at that and thought, that doesn't seem right.

The major problem I have with that now is when I read all my paperwork. It says that the reason the placement broke down was because of Steven's disruptive behaviour. Steven had a hard time settling into the family. It's all lies! That's not what happened! Yes, I was cheeky, but they were meant to support me. They were meant to love me as their own. I was abused in multiple ways.

I didn't tell the social worker anything. I was too scared. The family also threatened my mummy. They sent people over to her house because at that point I was only seeing my mummy once every six months. I vividly remember telling her that they had been hitting me, and she became visibly distressed, her eyes welling up with tears as she struggled to process the news. I think on one of the contact visits she must have shouted at them or something. They sent people round to my mummy's house to threaten her. They never admitted it but we know it was them because the people that turned up said something like, "don't ever go back to that house again, if you ever try to, we'll come round and sort you out."

I looked like I could have been their child. I looked like their son, so it seemed like I fitted in nicely. I went to the same school. My younger sister might have been jealous sometimes, I think, because I was quite a demanding child and that's when the wheels started to fall off.

One day, *mum* hauled me out of bed and told me to get in the bath. She shut the door and sat on the toilet next to me, made me take all my clothes off and said, "get in." I was in the bath, and I was trying to tell her, "I don't need you in here. I can do it by myself."

She said, "I don't know if you're going to clean yourself properly. I've got to make sure you clean yourself properly." She scrubbed my body with the sponge so forcefully that it felt like my skin might peel off, then she lathered soap into my hair. Since my hair was thick, the soap seeped painfully into my eyes, making them burn and water, but she didn't seem to notice or care. Each time she pushed my head under the water to rinse, I felt a jolt of fear, especially when she held me down for what felt like an eternity. My chest tightened, and my thoughts raced as I struggled for air. I panicked, flailing weakly, desperate to surface, but her grip held firm. When she finally pulled me back up, tears streamed down my face as I gasped for air. Her calm response chilled me further: "I was just trying to make sure the soap was out of your hair!"

It was a terrifying experience for me sadly this was something I endured more than once.

If I had been cheeky or I had asked for something from the shops and she didn't buy it for me, she'd say things like, "you've embarrassed me out here, I'll embarrass you when we get home."

There were many moments that made me feel out of place. One night, after my younger sister and I had gone to bed, I heard my foster *mum* quietly enter my sisters' room next door. She whispered softly, but I could still make out her words: "I think he's asleep. You can come back down now." Moments later, I heard my sister tiptoeing down the stairs. It hit me then. I wasn't part of their family. They waited for me to fall asleep so they could have their own time together.

Determined to see what was going on, I got out of bed and decided to follow. When I went downstairs, they were all in the lounge enjoying a TV show. My foster *mum* turned to me with a surprised look, her tone cold as she asked, "What are you doing here?"

I said, "Oh, Gemma's come down."

She said, "Don't worry about Gemma. Get back to bed."

So, I went back upstairs and got into bed.

I spent a lot of days in the six-weeks' holidays in my room. During term time, I had to come back from school and go straight to bed. I wasn't allowed to play out. I would only come down and have my dinner. If I was causing trouble, I had to pick whether to face punishment with the hanger or the wooden spoon.

One thing I noticed was that the dad and the son, were not around much. They seemed to always be out of the house. Now this is the tragedy, I was moved because of my race and the need for a father figure, yet I spent little time with this man. I spent most of the time with my new *mum,* Julie, and Gemma.

Also, I remember the whale movie, Free Willy, 1993. All the kids were getting excited about Free Willy coming out at the cinema and they had arranged to go and watch it as a family. What I don't understand is why she waited for me to get my coat on and walk to the front door, before saying, "where do you think you're going?"

I said, "What do you mean, we're going to the cinema?"

She went, "no, you're not coming, you've been naughty, naughty boys don't come."

Gemma asked with genuine concern, "Are you going to leave him by himself?"

She said, "yes, as long as the doors are locked, he's alright by himself."

They all went off to watch the movie without me. Gemma came back with a bit of popcorn that she'd saved for me. Even she knew what her mother did was wrong.

There was a holiday to Pontins. This was another poignant moment for me. As it turned out they had only booked six people into the chalet, Roger, Pat, and their three kids. They also had another family member come along as well So, we were approaching the entrance gate at Pontins, and they stopped the car and said to me, "you've got to go in the boot."

I was like, "why do I need to go in the boot?"

"Because they can't see the additional family member, we've only booked for six of us." I remember having to hide in the boot and that was a big thing for me. It cemented for me the fact that I was not a part of their family. There were always these subliminal messages sent.

One time I walked into the kitchen and she and her husband, Roger, were having an argument. She started saying, "It's him, he's rude, he's ruining this family."

I felt like a piece of shit to be honest with you. It felt like they could pick me up and just drop me whenever they liked. Mum would repeat, "You know, you're not making it work in this family." It seemed like a job interview to become a son in the family, but I didn't meet the qualifications, so I was dismissed.

It was two years of hell, even on the day I was leaving them, *mum* didn't even see me off. "Because this hasn't worked, they will move you to a children's home, and you'll get bullied. It's your fault. You haven't made this work and that's why you're going to live in a children's home." She told me a few days before.

In summer 1994, it was decided the family could no longer meet my behavioural and emotional needs, and so I was moved into my first children's home, Sutton Road in Erdington, Birmingham.

Four

Dave

The children's home was on Sutton Road in Erdington, Birmingham. A lot of the children's homes back then were named after the road they were on.

So, Sutton Road is where I met Dave, he was a care worker in the home and the person I regard as my *power of one*. I would like to dedicate this chapter to Dave.

When I first arrived at Sutton Road Children's Home, I was scared and anxious. I was coming from an abusive home with my Forever Family. I had in the back of my mind the words my new *mum* had said to me. Until this point, I knew nothing about life in a children's home. I thought, *I'm going to get hurt, I'm going to get bullied, but I'm already coming from a place where I was hurt and bullied by my foster mum.*

I was distraught and I was fearful, plus a hint of anticipation. I was going in there with other children that felt the same way as I did.

There were approximately 14 of us. It was a 22-bed home, the largest children's home in Birmingham at the time. It was a big house with many rooms. The garden looked like a field. I had never been anywhere like this before. They had three tractor tyres, large, medium and small, in the ground for us to run along and sit in, whatever we wanted to do with them. We would play hide and seek. There was a big fence. Loads of room we would run around all the time. I was warming more to the ways of Sutton Road I guess.

I moved in close to the weekend with only 70p. We got pocket money for chores or good behaviour and spent it on sweets and toys from Woolworths on Erdington High Street. We loved visiting Sega World, an arcade above Blockbuster.

I felt like I was on the scrapheap; it felt like I'd been dumped. On Christmas morning in 1994, I was opening presents provided by the local authority, reflecting on the circumstances. The magical Christmases of my early life had faded to just memories, leaving me feeling a profound sense of sadness and numbness. The joy and wonder that once filled those holiday mornings were replaced by a hollow emptiness, as I struggled to reconcile the past with the present reality.

There's a symbolic picture of me on the floor in the children's home in a few pages.

To say I was mischievous would be an understatement. My antics often involved performing exaggerated gestures, making silly faces, or creating humorous scenarios to entertain my peers. I discovered that drawing laughter from others gave me a sense of connection and ease in an otherwise challenging environment.

Dave remains one of the most unforgettable figures from my time at Sutton Road. Unlike anyone else, Dave had this unmatched ability to connect with the children on a level that transcended the typical responsibilities of a care worker. When I say he was different, I mean he truly stood out in his approach to nurturing and engaging us. He wasn't just there to oversee the day-to-day or enforce rules; he brought life, colour, and creativity into our world.

Dave had this remarkable knack for turning ordinary moments into something magical. He would bring in instruments and paints, encouraging us to express ourselves creatively. I still vividly remember the gigantic mural he painted on the wall, filled with Disney characters like Mickey Mouse and Donald Duck. It wasn't just a decoration; it was a symbol of his dedication to making our environment lively and uplifting. He made us feel like we mattered, that we were part of something special.

Dave was all about getting us involved in hands-on activities. Whether it was cooking, baking cakes, or conker picking, he always found ways to engage us. His enthusiasm was infectious. Unlike other staff members who would sit down to watch TV with us or eat dinner in a more regimented manner, Dave was constantly present and available. He was proactive, thoughtful, and genuinely invested in our happiness and well-being.

Bedtime was another time when Dave's unique spirit shone through. He would read us stories, a simple gesture, but one that carried so much warmth and care. There's a story he told me much later that still resonates deeply. One night, while he was preparing to read me a bedtime story, I apparently jumped up on top of my wardrobe and started making monkey noises. Dave, with his characteristic patience and humour, said, "Steve, come on, get down. I'm going to read this story to you." When I finally settled into bed, I asked him, "Will you be my dad?" That question, he told me in later years, took him aback. He didn't know what to say at the time, but it speaks volumes about the kind of relationship he fostered with us. To me, Dave wasn't just a care worker; he was a father figure, someone I gravitated toward naturally.

All the children loved Dave. He had this magnetic quality that drew us to him, and he became a source of comfort and joy in a time when those feelings were often hard to come by. While there was other male staff members Ken, Charles and Michael all of whom carried their own unique strengths, something was truly special about Dave. He wasn't just a support worker; he was a pillar of kindness and creativity in our lives, someone who made a lasting impact that I hold with me to this day.

One evening, Dave told me to stop misbehaving at the table and to eat my dinner nicely so everyone else could eat in peace. Then in that moment, I placed my cutlery down, smiled at Dave and said, *"Me and Dave crack up like cracker on a Christmas tree."* In that moment Dave couldn't help but laugh, at a time he was trying to be serious. This is a memory that Dave and I hold dearly as it would go onto live with us in the later years when we reconnect beyond the walls of the care system.

Me and Dave Crack Up Like Cracker on a Christmas Tree

Drip By Drip Day By Day

Steven Russell

Drip By Drip Day By Day

I had to leave Hall Green Primary school and started attending Wylde Green Primary School, when I moved into Sutton Road. I had been at Hall Green for years four and five. I was now in year six, you have to bear in mind, that's the final year in primary school so the other children had been together for so many years from nursery to infants, to juniors. So, me walking into year six as a new child was extremely hard. It was a classic child in care situation.

On my first day at Wylde Green, Ken, who was the manager of Sutton Road, said, "I'll take you to school."

I just remember saying to him when we got there, "can you stay with me for the day?"

He said, "No I can't stay with you but I'll make sure you get in ok and we will get someone to collect you later."

This is the life of a child in care. This is what happens. When they are moved out of the area, they have to move schools. The ramifications of that are, you've got to lose friends, make friends, start again. It tears you apart inside. You just don't have any faith in people. I couldn't set down any roots. There was no point, and I had absolutely no control at all.

At Wylde Green Primary School, they had their main school building and then they had another room like an annexe over the road and that's where the year six was based.

I stepped out of the school's reception, feeling nervous, as the teacher smiled and said, "Let's go meet your new classmates." We crossed the road and walked into the year six classroom. It felt like an American movie everything froze, heads turned, and all eyes were suddenly on me. That was a horrible feeling.

I say to a lot of the kids I work with now, when you're starting a new school, it's a big thing. You've got to appreciate it's not an easy thing to do.

Starting at a new school can feel like being dropped in the middle of a dense jungle, where every face is unfamiliar, and every rule is unknown. For children in care, this experience often comes with added layers, leaving behind friends, adapting to a new environment, and navigating the unavoidable sense of uncertainty.

I vividly remember those first moments with the teacher guiding me across the road to my new classroom. My heartbeat echoed in my ears, each step feeling heavier than the last. The classroom was bright with colourful posters on the walls, but the stares from students were what I noticed most. It wasn't hostility, no, it was curiosity the kind of curiosity that makes you hyper-aware of every movement you make. For a moment, I wanted to retreat, to run back into the safety of the reception area. But I knew I couldn't.

That day marked the beginning of an uphill climb, but it also set the stage for something unexpected. Over time, small gestures began to turn the tide. A shared joke over lunch, a game of football on the playground, and the look of approval from classmates when I answered a tricky question correctly. All of these moments started to stitch together a sense of belonging.

Slowly but surely, I learned that even in unfamiliar places, connections could be made, and roots could be planted even if only for a little while. It was during this time that I formed a meaningful friendship with Timmy, a boy who intrigued me from the start. Timmy bore a striking resemblance to me; his skin was of a similar complexion. He sported neat dreadlocks, a characteristic shared by his older brother and father. Timmy's family was welcoming and warm, often inviting me over to their home to share meals.

Timmy himself was exceptional in many ways. He was not only kind-hearted but also an incredibly talented football player, so much so that he had trials with West Bromwich Albion. His skill on the field earned admiration from both classmates and teachers, but what I valued most was his unwavering support. Timmy became my protector at school, ensuring that no one bothered me or made me feel out of place. It was as if he instinctively understood the challenges I faced and made it his mission to shield me from them.

Looking back, I realise how fortunate I was to have someone like Timmy by my side. Throughout my life, it seems there has always been someone who stepped up to befriend me and offer their guidance and support. Whether it was a classmate standing up for me or a peer reaching out with kindness, these connections have been invaluable.

We had a staff member named Beverly who worked the night shift to assist any children needing support while the daytime staff rested. We adored Beverly, especially because her son was Carlton Palmer, a professional footballer. When he played for Leeds, she would bring in signed pictures of him, which we found so exciting.

Also, Julie, who was a member of staff, had friends who worked over at Villa Park. I'm a big Villa fan. They knew she worked in a children's home, so they would give her free tickets for the games. We were always going down to Villa Park as kids; we even got to see Dwight Yorke. After a game, he came to the main gate where the players would drive out. He had a Rover car, I think Villa was sponsored by Rover and I said, "Can I hold your car keys?"

He replied, "As long as you don't run off with them." I gave him his keys back, and he asked, "How do you think we played today?"

I told Dwight Yorke, "Ah, you play much better when you're not wearing white boots." He didn't wear the white boots again after that!

I went to more Villa games as a child than I do as an adult. I can't even count how many games we went to. I became immersed in it, and because we were all going together, it was so much fun. Once in the stadium, you know the chants? There was a player called Savo Milošević, and the song was, "When you hear me say, boom, boom, boom, let me hear you say Savo, Savo." I stood up on my chair and started singing. The next thing I knew, the whole stadium started singing it. Great times.

When we think about growing up in care, it's not all doom and gloom. Yes, there are lots of emotions there and sleepless nights, but in the grand scheme, the staff did what they could to get us out and about, camping trips, the park, just going out and about doing things. I suffered no abuse in the care homes from the staff. I had some problems with the other children there, but that was to be expected.

There were so many children coming through the home that we would have to share bedrooms. Sutton Road was mixed girls and boys. At the home, relationships between the boys and girls were common. We would engage in sexual experimentation with each other. Occasionally we'd find discarded cigarettes and smoke them in our rooms. We were young kids. We didn't really know what we were doing, and the supervision wasn't great.

We would be upstairs for hours, losing ourselves in the world we had carved out of chaos. At times, the staff would come looking for us, their voices carrying a mix of concern and resignation. But the truth was, they didn't always know what to say or do; it seemed easier for them to let us figure out things on our own.

Then there were the days when we'd escape to the nearby park, laughing and running until the sky turned to twilight. Inevitably, the staff would grow worried and call the police, setting off a search that was more ritualistic than urgent. We'd dart through the Lyndhurst estate, drawing invisible maps of freedom in places where we weren't supposed to be. Those fleeting moments felt like defiance, but looking back, they were the quiet rebellions of children searching for a place to belong.

Five

Little Steven's voice

Primarily, a child needs to be loved and have their basic physiological needs met, according to Maslow's Hierarchy of Needs. So, the top sections in Maslow's theory regarding Belonging, Esteem, and Self-Actualisation were met, in part, in my first foster home with Pat. My cultural needs could all have been addressed through different interventions by social workers, as Pat definitely provided for my physiological, safety needs and the need for love and security.

I feel really sad at this moment, thinking about being taken away from Pat's care because I was happy. I was in a loving, nurturing environment that was just the best for me, only to be moved and abused terribly.

While I was living in Sutton Road, my social worker was trying to find another foster home for me, and I read in my paperwork a family had been identified in Wales. However, my social worker said that Steven needs older siblings. He needs individual attention, which families with older siblings are better at providing. Apparently, this family in Wales had two children around my age. Can you imagine that? That's how life works in the care system. Imagine if those children were older, I would have most likely ended up moving to Wales. My life would have taken a different direction, and again, I don't know what my life would have looked like today. I would have been living in Wales as a 12-year-old.

The essence of a child in care is that we are like the leaves in the wind never knowing where we're going; all we know is that we're blowing around this place they call the care system. Often, it's like we are that little white ball on a roulette wheel waiting to find out the number of the new address where we will be living.

A young person I once mentored decided to write a song called "Two Leaves in the Wind."

In the beginning, you're attached to your family tree, and then the winds of uncertainty and pain come along, and leaves get blown off. Your leaf is just blowing around; the wind stops for a little bit, and your leaf lands on someone's doorstep. This new place you have to call home, form new attachments, new roots, new relationships. And all of a sudden, the winds begin to blow again, sometimes quickly turning into a

tornado. Whoosh, you're off again, and you don't know where you're going to land.

My leaf could have gone to Wales. Imagine that! Me waking up in Wales to begin a whole new journey.

My social worker came to visit me at Sutton Road and told me, "There might be a chance for you to go back to live with Pat, but I can't make any promises." She told me it would have to go to court, and the judge would decide.

I asked her, "Can I write a letter to the judge to maybe persuade him to let me go live back with Pat?"

She said, "You can write your letter if you want to, that's no problem."

So, I wrote this letter:

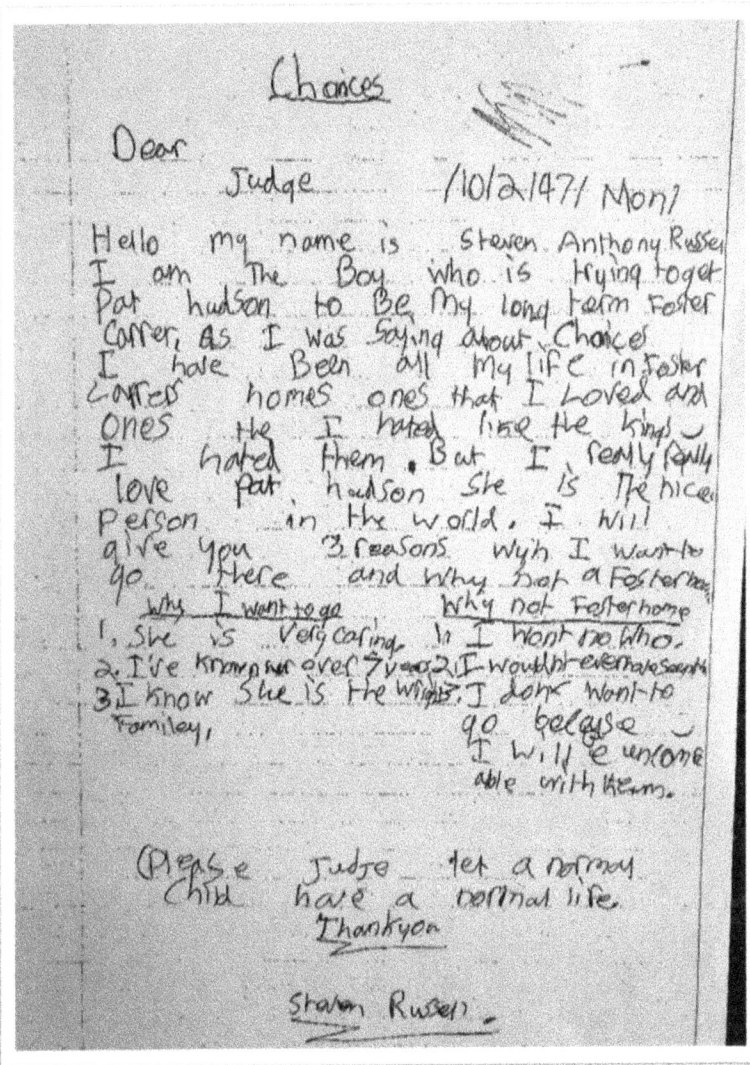

Choices   10/2/97/Mon

Dear Judge

My name is Steven Anthony Russell. The boy who is trying to get Pat Hudson to be my long-term foster carer, as I was saying about Choices I have been all my life in foster carers homes, ones that I loved and ones that I hated like the "*Forever family.*" I hated them but I really really love Pat Hudson, she is the nicest person in the world. I will give you three reasons why I want to go there and not the foster home.

<u>Why I want to go to Pat's:</u>

1. She is very caring

2. I've known her over seven years

3. I know she is the right family

<u>Why not go to new foster home:</u>

1. I won't know who

2. I wouldn't ever have seen them

3. I don't want to go because I will be uncomfortable with them.

Please judge, let a normal child have a normal life. Thank you - Steven Russell.

I suppose it's important to mention that a 12-year-old Steven has written this letter hoping he goes back to live with Pat his loving foster mother.

Thankfully the judge agreed I could return to Pat's care. She was now living in Great Barr. The first few months were brilliant, but by that time, because of the two years I'd suffered with the forever family and the move to Sutton Road, I was slowly releasing the trauma I had experienced to and around someone I felt safe with in Pat.

I was in pain, and my behaviour took a troubling turn. I began exhibiting signs of bullying, aggression, and anger. There were moments where my actions reflected the confusion and trauma I carried, with some of it manifesting in inappropriate and sexualised behaviour. These behaviours, though they were cries for help, placed an unbearable strain on our relationship. Pat faced an agonising decision that would ultimately lead to my removal from her care.

I often did not want to eat my meals, I wanted to do whatever I wanted and when I wanted.

Pat taught me a valuable lesson. I complained that I didn't want to have dinner; I wanted to eat sweets. I came back from school and she'd put sweets on my dinner plate. I thought this was great, so I ate the sweets. Later on, my stomach started hurting. I said, "Is there any food?"

"No!" She said, "Well you didn't want your dinner!"

The pain surfaced in ways that neither Pat nor I could fully control. Despite her immense care and love, Pat did everything she could for about a year, tirelessly trying to manage the overwhelming challenges I presented. However, as time passed, it became evident that she struggled to maintain trust in me around the other children she fostered.

It was a challenging and bewildering period in my life, the abuse, the exposure and trauma in the years I lived away from Pat had damaged me. I grappled with questions I did not yet have the tools to answer.

Drip By Drip Day By Day

Six

Removed

During my time in Year 7, while living with Pat, I had a routine of taking a taxi every day from Kingstanding to Castle Vale Comprehensive School. One particular afternoon, as I returned home, I noticed my social worker's car parked outside. Curious and slightly uneasy, I went inside and she asked me to change out of my school uniform and come downstairs for a conversation. When I returned, she shared the difficult news: "We've had to make a tough decision. Pat has been struggling to manage your behaviours, and it's been decided that you will need to move to another children's home."

I thought I would have more time to adjust, but within just a week, I found myself heading to St Athans Croft Children's Home. Unlike Sutton Road, St Athans Croft was an all-boys home located in Castle Vale. Before stepping into my social worker's car, I went back to Pat for one last hug. I held onto her tightly, telling her I loved her while my heart felt like it was breaking into pieces. I didn't want to let go, but I had no choice. At that point, I had to accept the decision and move on, a pattern that seemed to define my life before I had even reached my teenage years.

I left a cassette tape under my pillow with an emotional message for Pat and Kate where I told them, *"I will miss you so much, I am sorry for my behaviour and I wish I could stay with you. I look forward to seeing you again one day. Thank you for being there for me and I hope you will write to me in my new home. I love you all very much."*

Here's a decision that makes absolutely no sense! When I moved to the children's home, I was transferred to a new school, Cardinal Wiseman, located in Kingstanding. Ironically, while living in Kingstanding, I attended a school in Castle Vale. Now that I was residing in Castle Vale, I was sent to a school in Kingstanding. The most absurd part was that Castle Vale School, where I had studied in Year 7 and had many friends, was literally right next to the children's home. Instead of attending the nearby school, I had to walk past it every day to catch a bus into Birmingham city centre and then transfer to another bus to Kingstanding. I had to repeat this journey daily. It's hard not to wonder, how does this even make sense?

As I experienced at Sutton Road, sharing my space with others often felt overwhelming and uncomfortable. I struggled to adjust to the communal nature of living arrangements, especially after being accustomed to the familiarity of a family home. The thought of sharing with other children felt intrusive, and at times, it was undeniably unpleasant. While the staff tried to provide some autonomy by allowing us to choose our roommates, as long as there was mutual agreement, it rarely made the situation feel easier or more bearable. The environment itself felt far removed from the stability and warmth I had once known.

When I moved to St Athans Croft, the pattern repeated itself. There, I met Nathan, another boy who reminded me of myself in many ways. Nathan had a similar appearance to me and an easy-going nature that made him approachable. Much like Timmy, Nathan took me under his wing, offering companionship and a sense of belonging during my time there.

These friendships, forged in the midst of uncertainty and change, were the threads that kept me grounded. They reminded me that even in the most unfamiliar environments, there was always the possibility of connection, understanding, and hope.

In primary school, I didn't mind people knowing that I lived in care. It was something I accepted without much thought, and the simplicity of childhood shielded me from many of the harsher judgments. But when I got to secondary school, everything changed. Suddenly, the idea of being in care became a source of shame, something that others would weaponise against me. The whispers, the side glances, and the cruel jabs from classmates cut into me in ways I didn't know how to navigate.

On the Castle Vale estate, there was a gang called the Green Box Crew, a notorious group of around thirty kids who ruled with intimidation and fear. They stole, they fought, and they left many of us walking on eggshells. Word spread quickly among them and others that I lived at St Athans Croft, the children's home nestled within the estate. It was almost impossible to keep that part of my life private, and its exposure felt like a constant spotlight on my vulnerabilities.

By the age of 13 or 14, the awareness of how others perceived me weighed heavily on my shoulders. I desperately wanted to keep my life in care a secret, to blend in and just be "normal" like everyone else. But the reality of that wish felt elusive, like a shadow I couldn't outrun. Each day brought reminders of the label I carried, and I worked tirelessly to keep some semblance of independence and dignity in the face of a world that often seemed determined to remind me of my differences.

When people asked where I lived, I often said I stayed with my aunt and uncle, deliberately avoiding the truth—that I lived in care. Admitting this felt too raw, too vulnerable, and too open to ridicule. The children's home, centrally located on Castle Vale, felt like a fortress under siege. It wasn't just a place where I slept; it was a battleground of whispers, judgments, and, at times, outright hostility.

The gang from the estate often made that hostility known. They would come to the home, shouting crude taunts, throwing bricks at the windows as though they were breaking into my inner world. The home had to replace the shattered glass with Perspex windows, a stark reminder that even the walls meant to protect us couldn't hold back the outside cruelty. And then there was the song. That haunting, mocking chant they sang as they passed by: "Where's ya Mamma gone? Where's ya Mamma gone?" The rhythm of it lingered in the air long after they'd stopped, like an unwelcome echo. At the time, I hardened myself against it, brushing it off like dirt on my shoes, but now, as I reflect, I realise how deeply it cut.

It wasn't just the attacks from the outside that shaped me; it was the kaleidoscope of experiences within those walls. Nights spent longing for something stable, something mine, clashed with moments of forced camaraderie. The communal living arrangements, the shared spaces, and the sheer number of faces coming and going left me with a sense of chaos that was hard to shake. Yet somehow, amidst the turmoil, I found fragments of resilience.

Looking back, I see the good, the bad, and the utterly heartbreaking moments that became the foundation of who I am today.

It's a double-edged sword. On one side, it's caused me to develop disorganised attachments. A fractured sense of trust that leaves me questioning the intentions of those around me. The inability to fully rely on others has been a lingering wound, a shadow cast over my connections with people. I find myself grappling with the uncertainty of who I can trust, and this has made forming deep, meaningful relationships a challenge. It's quite damaging in that respect, creating barriers that seem almost impossible to break down.

Yet, on the other side, this very exposure to a multitude of personalities and behaviours has given me a keen insight into human nature. Being privy to so many different characters throughout my life has honed my ability to read people, to understand their motivations, and to gauge their authenticity. This skill has become a kind of armour, a tool that allows me to navigate social situations with a heightened sense of perception. In a way, it's helped me, turning adversity into an unexpected advantage.

The juxtaposition of these two outcomes, a fractured sense of trust alongside an ability to understand people deeply, paints a complex picture. While it's bittersweet, it has shaped the way I approach the world, equipping me with resilience and insight, even if accompanied by a quiet longing for the simplicity of unguarded trust.

Seven

Chameleon

I've often thought of myself as a chameleon, effortlessly adapting to various groups, whether it was hanging out with the guys on the road, surrounded by the smoke of cannabis and casual banter. Or mingling with people in suburban Sutton Coldfield. This adaptability stems from the diverse experiences I've lived through. Take Pat, for example: during my early childhood (ages 1-7), I lived with roughly 100 children, a figure Pat also remembers vividly due to the transient nature of their short-term respite care stays. The constant flow of children created a chaotic yet oddly familiar rhythm in the house.

If you could see the countless photos of me with children from all backgrounds, White, Black, Asian, and of every age, you would understand how deeply ingrained my ability to navigate different social settings has evolved. Yet there's a flip side to this. My natural inclination veers towards solitude and isolation. While I enjoy being around people, I find my true solace when I'm alone. This duality often leaves me feeling socially conflicted.

Even now, I question how I've managed to stand on a stage and share my life experiences with an audience of 600 people. *How did I get to this point? How did it happen?* I know the answer lies in the stories, the backdrop of my life that gives weight to my words. It's not something I could achieve with a generic PowerPoint presentation. True, I do use PowerPoints, but they're crafted with intention, designed to complement my narrative.

When I think about confidence and how I've cultivated it, two words come to mind: self and belief. I believe in myself with extraordinary tenacity, so much so that at times it has spilled over into cockiness and arrogance. But that's just part of who I am, someone who believes they know best.

Having mastered the balance between confidence and arrogance, I now approach performances with an air of calmness and ease. Whether addressing an audience of 5,000 or engaging in a casual Zoom call with someone like Marcia, my publisher, I strive to remain authentic to who I am. I can only be Steven, raw, real, and relatable.

From a young age, I learned that the only person I could truly depend on was myself. Though I had many people around me, Daves, Pats, Adams, compassionate and loving individuals they couldn't fill the emotional void I carried.

Even now, as I edge closer to 40, it remains hard to admit, but I still feel a certain emotional distance from those closest to me. It's an uncomfortable truth; one I occasionally sugarcoat. We all do it, don't we? Exaggerating and compensating to mask the unvarnished reality. The truth isn't always pretty.

I love my children deeply and unconditionally. For them, I would make any sacrifice without hesitation. I do everything I can to show my love, yet there's still a psychological and emotional void. That void carries a label of selfishness, and it stings because I don't want to be perceived that way. But I understand why. Little Steven reminds me, "You didn't choose to become selfish, it's how your experiences have wired and conditioned you." My fallback is crystal clear: Steven has to look after himself.

Looking back, friendships from my childhood feel transient. They were there for a while, but then I had to leave and they became distant memories. It's soul-crushing to admit that I don't have friends from that time. But with this book, my goal has always been to leave no stone unturned.

I could easily gloss over the pain and say I became who I am today because of my adverse childhood experiences. While that's true, it doesn't tell the whole story. We like to skip those uncomfortable pages. The ones that hurt most to remember.

Drip By Drip Day By Day

Eight

A Black and White World

The Weight of a Question
"What are ya?"

That was the question that followed me everywhere. People seemed to ask it before anything else, before they even bothered to learn my name. It didn't matter where I was, in the playground, at school, or even at the care home. It hung in the air, unspoken in some cases but always felt, like the sound of a distant train you can't quite see.

The answers people offered up for me were endless. Half-caste, mixed-race, dual heritage, biracial. But there was one term, one label, that no one handed me. No one ever called me "half-white." My mum, who was white, always seemed to vanish into the background of my identity, as though her part in creating me wasn't worth acknowledging.

Adults didn't just ask about my identity; they decided it for me. "You're more black, though, aren't you?" they'd say, referencing my dad's skin tone as if that was the only detail that mattered. There was this strange assumption that my identity could be split into percentages, weighed up, and then neatly filed away.

But I didn't want to play their game. I couldn't. Race, as I saw it even as a kid in the care system isn't something you pick and subscribe to. It's a man-made concept, carved into the walls of society like graffiti no one bothers to scrub off. A construct we've all been forced to live under, whether we like it or not.

And I didn't like it.

Mixed Faces in Mixed Places

Growing up in the care system, I was already dealing with being the odd one out in new homes, new schools, and new neighbourhoods. But my so-called identity threw an extra layer on top of all that this constant sense of not quite fitting in, anywhere. The black kids would say I was too light to truly be one of them. "You're not properly black, though," Jermaine once sneered after I mentioned that I liked Bob Marley.

The white kids didn't make it easier. "You're not really one of us either," Lewis told me when I asked to join their football game. Either side I turned to, the answer was the same in different words. I wasn't enough. Too dark to be one thing; too light to be the other.

Why did everything have to be about my skin tone, my heritage, or where I fit? Why did people assume that every choice I made was tied to something bigger, something about race? No matter what I liked, what I did, or where I went, it all came back to the same thing. Identity was a puzzle other people were determined to solve for me.

It didn't just end with opinions, though. It was built into the systems around me, always forcing me to choose. Every form I filled out, every box I had to tick, was another reminder that no one wanted to see me as just Steven. "Black or white? Choose one." And when they added "other" to the list, it felt just as bad. Like all they could say was, "You don't fit, so here's a catch-all category for people we don't know what to do with."

Even as a child, I couldn't make sense of this obsession with putting people into boxes. I'd lie awake at night, staring at the shadows on the ceiling of my care home bedroom, wondering why it all mattered so much. Why couldn't I just *be*?

The Layers of Belonging

What made navigating the care system even harder was the way this identity crisis impacted every interaction, every relationship. Living in care strips you of comfort and control. You're already fumbling through a life filled with new faces, strict routines, and constant change. Add in society's demands for you to answer questions about who you are, and the weight becomes unbearable.

At ten years old, I was already feeling the pull of racism, colourism, and unconscious bias. Racism was the obvious one. The casual remarks, the looks. I knew what that was. Colourism, on the other hand, was trickier to spot, but it found its way into conversations. "Best of both worlds", they called it, you should think yourself lucky Steven, you get to be both black and white at the same time.

Then there's unconscious bias, where people didn't even realise, they were treating me differently. Care staff, teachers, even other children would judge me before I even said a word. And the message was always the same, loud and clear, no matter how softly it was delivered. You don't belong.

Running the Race of Racism

We seem to live in a society today where atrocities and horrendous acts of violence aren't defined by a person's race, ethnicity, or skin colour but by what they have done and the character of their actions. However, the questions people ask, still portray an obsession with identity. I find it deeply troubling that after an act of savagery, like the terrible incident I watched unfold on the news, one of the first things so many people want to know is "What's their race? Are they a migrant?"

That particular news story has stayed with me. A man had driven his car through a crowd of people, a violent and barbaric act. But what stood out to me most was when the officer reporting on the incident made it very clear to the public that the perpetrator was a white British male. Why did that need saying? Because, in today's society, had this person been from anywhere else, had they been of a different ethnicity, our streets would have erupted in chaos. Marches would have spilled onto the roads, fuelled by organisations like the EDL, spreading anger and division.

It's almost as if people accept violence or savagery more readily if it comes from someone who looks and sounds like them. Isn't that empty? Isn't that sad? We've got to the point where we're more concerned about *who* committed an atrocity than about the atrocity itself. It's dehumanising. It reduces tragedies to cheap talking points, strips them of the pain and suffering involved, and instead reroutes the focus to race, migration status, or skin colour.

But does it even matter? If someone drives a car into a crowd, why does their ethnicity change the tragedy? Why does society care less about the action itself based on who committed it? These are the questions that haunt me as I look at the world and its obsession with labels, boxes, and definitions that divide us before we've even had the chance to find common ground.

A New Way Forward

At the heart of it all, I knew this much, I didn't want to carry other people's ideas of identity anymore. I was tired of holding their assumptions, their questions, their debates. I was just Steven. Not black. Not white. Not *other*.

The world might not be ready for that kind of simplicity, but I had to believe it was possible. I had to believe that one day, we could move beyond skin colour and celebrate the complex, messy, human beauty we all carry.

What if we could stop crafting boxes and start seeing each other for who we really are? It's a question I carry with me every day, and one I hope we'll all take time to answer.

Nine

Rejection, The Labels

Shame, letting people down. I believe that being a good parent starts with having good parents who can serve as your blueprint for parenting. People say, "My parents weren't perfect, but their love and support gave me the confidence to face parenthood without fear." I never had that. I never had a good enough parent. I had 10 foster homes, different care homes and five schools. So chaotic, disjointed, and dysregulated. I was always going to have the imprint of that life on my parenting style. Even though me and Laura, my children's mother, aren't together anymore, I work hard every single day to remind my kids that I love them. Of course, I sometimes fall short. I go to bed sometimes kicking myself because I don't remember if I have told my kids that I love them today. We all grapple with the question. "Am I good enough?"

I went from the "Forever family" to Sutton Road, from Sutton Road back to Pat's and then to St Athan. On the day that I left Pat's, my social worker came to pick me up and move me. It was during the day, after school. When I arrived home, we had KFC for dinner, which was usually a special treat. It turned out to be my last meal, much like the last meal of a condemned man.

Inside me there was a fear. Every time I had to move it would be a night of crying and gut-wrenching bawling. The first night was always filled with tears. My blue bear Elias was the only one I shared these moments with. He was with me throughout my childhood years, the only stable thing in my life. Elias my blue bear was always with me to soak up the tears.

After a move, the days turned into weeks, and I would gradually acclimatise to my surroundings and learnt more of how to camouflage myself from threats, real or perceived. Before I knew it, I was part of and amid the throng of young testosterone. At St Athan's there was Nathen, Jeremy, Adrian, Simon, and Jason. *All the Boys!* Some of us didn't get on and we got into fights and things like that. Nathen was the main one there and because he took a liking to me, no one messed around with me.

At St Athan's we had to share rooms. The rooms were basic. The thing I remember is that each room had a sink in it.

The first time I tried a cigarette was with Simon, he was teaching me how to smoke, hold it and inhale it. I couldn't, I don't know how to inhale it. I started to inhale but then my body started to naturally reject it, I was sick and dizzy, my body was saying this isn't for me. Because I was living with these guys every day, I ended up trying it again and before you know it I'm a smoker, even cannabis. When she found out, my mum was upset about it, but since we didn't get along, I would tell her to, "F off!"

Although we smoked with the staff in those days, they weren't allowed to provide us with cigarettes. They used to say, "I can't hand you the cigarette but I can drop it on the floor." I know it was wrong but it helped us build a relationship with them, through our shared addiction. I recall fun times out on trips in the staff cars.

I also spent a lot of time with *All the Boys* walking around the estate and causing trouble. I used to like fire so I would burn things, break car windows, post fireworks through people's letter boxes. That was fun…madness, we got up to madness. Ransacking the house and not going to sleep.

The good thing was that the local lads would come round with their systems and microphones, and we would rap in the lounge. I really enjoyed that, even some of the staff would jump on the mic. That's how I learnt how to do a little rapping. It was my link worker who I'm connected to now; we met up for some food not too long ago. So, my key worker made sure I had all my personal effects, money, and family contact.

My relationship with my mum changed as I grew older; my teenage years brought more independence and less compliance. So, when I got like 13 or 14, it was a middle finger to my mum. I'm doing what I want to do.

My friend Pete who moved in with me a couple of years later, and we had a blast going to Birmingham to buy crazy stuff like padlocks, chains, sweets, and random items from Poundland for a pound. We were too young to buy cigarettes and so had some fun times, trying to get our hands on cigarettes. There was a local bus driver called Jim who sold them. Sometimes we would stand outside the shops and ask adults to buy us some cigarettes. This was a lot of fun watching how different people would react. Even our next-door neighbours would let us do their garden for a pack of cigarettes.

When I was coming back from school, I got run over and thought I was going to die. The car hit me on my side and I flew up, then eventually landed with a head-butt to the curb. I had to do something like a police statement, but I couldn't remember the car details.

The girls in the neighbourhood were quick to find out when a new boy moved into the boys' home, and they would often gather to get a closer look at the newcomer. The rest is crude and we don't need to know about that.

The day I was run over marked one of the most vivid memories from that chaotic chapter of my life. I remember walking back from school, my mind elsewhere, as it so often was, when the car came out of nowhere. The impact hit me hard on the side, launching me into the air before I landed painfully on the curb, my head smashing against the pavement in one brutal moment. Everything happened in a blur, faces crowding around me, murmurs of concern, and the piercing pain that made it impossible to think straight.

Later, I was asked to provide a police statement about the incident, but the details were hazy. The make of the car, its colour, everything had been swallowed by the chaos of the moment. All I could remember was the overwhelming shock and a strange sort of resignation, thinking, "This is it. This is how it ends." But it didn't end there, and that night, as I lay in bed nursing my bruises, I felt a strange clarity: life was unpredictable, uncontrollable, and I would have to learn to live with its uncertainties.

Life at the boys' home brought its own set of unpredictable encounters and complications. Whenever a new boy arrived, it was like a ripple in a pond, everyone noticed, especially the girls from the surrounding neighbourhood. Word spread fast, and they'd come by, curious to see the newcomer, their giggles and glances adding a touch of excitement to an otherwise routine existence. The interactions that followed were often crude, fuelled by the raw energy of teenage years and the lack of boundaries that seemed to govern those moments. These fleeting encounters were a part of the madness that surrounded us, a mix of curiosity, rebellion, and the search for connection in a world that often felt disconnected.

Looking back, those days were a whirlwind of experiences, some reckless, some painful, and others absurdly amusing. They shaped who I was in ways I couldn't fully understand at the time, leaving me with stories that, while chaotic, were uniquely mine.

Ten

The Search for Belonging

As you can imagine by now, my trust in being a part of a family was pretty much non-existent. Not only did I struggle with the concept of a family, but I also despised it. I loathed it. I was my family; all I needed was me, myself, and I. The more moves a child has through multiple families, the more chance this dwindling effect will happen—this idea that you weren't good enough for family one, two, three, and so on.

So, when my keyworker Dino from St Athan's children's home asked if I would be willing to give foster care another go, my initial answer was, "Forget that." All I wanted to do was get to sixteen, sign myself out of care, and live by myself. This is what I had watched the older lads in the home do, and so that is exactly what I thought would be best for me.

At the time Dino asked me this, I was thirteen years of age, and so I thought, "Three more years, and I can go and live my best life." Dino told me my social worker had identified a potential family—specialist teenage foster carers that could be a good fit for me. He could see that I was quite hesitant, and then he said, "Why don't you just meet them? If you don't feel it would be a good idea to pursue this, then of course you can say no and carry on as you are. But at least meet them to see whether they might be a good option."

I decided to take on board Dino's points, and so the visit was set up. Eunice and Neville came to the home to visit me. At first, I was a little bit shy, but the first thing I noticed about them was this warm energy. It's the same warm energy that I use to describe people like Adam, Dave, and Pat. It's the unspoken word. It's the friendly smile. It's the warm atmosphere. It's the non-threatening body language.

I remember Neville saying, "Hello, you must be Steven. My name's Neville," in his deep Jamaican tone of voice. It was different. I'd always been used to white and mixed-race families. This was new. Eunice had such a calming nature and could probably see that I was a bit nervous, so she said, "Why don't you come for dinner? Come and see the house. And if it's not for you, then we can bring you back." There was no expectation, no false promises, no stern tone. Just open arms, open hands, and what sounded like an open door to a potential opportunity.

I remember one day after school, I was taken over to their home in Erdington, which was quite a familiar area, although this particular part wasn't as familiar—Witton Lodge Road, where the number 7 and number 65 buses drive. The first thing I noticed when I walked into the house was the smell of food. Although I couldn't tell what type of food it was, it was just a beautiful smell, a smell that I would become very familiar with. The walls were well-decorated with family photos and a crucifix. Eunice and Neville were religious, but not the type to rub it in your face; they just had their own faith in God.

They showed me around the house and showed me the bedroom that I could potentially be in if I chose to move in. The lounge was big, and they had one of those TVs where you had to put a pound coin in it to keep it going. They had a wonderful kitchen, a big stove, a lovely conservatory area, a nice garden, a good bathroom, and a lovely veranda on the front that you could sit out on in the summertime and watch the traffic and the world go by.

There was something about this house that made me feel like I was home, even though I hadn't made any decision to make this my home.

We sat down for dinner—me, Eunice, and Neville. The food smelled nice, but I wasn't sure what it was. I'd explained to Eunice that my main diet consisted of burgers, chips, chicken nuggets, beans, eggs, and a full English breakfast.

I'd never been introduced to mutton and rice, ackee and saltfish, dumplings, or fried chicken until now.

So, I'm sat there at the table with my cap on, about to tuck into what seemed to be gorgeous food, when a stern voice from the end of the table—Neville—said, "Take your hat off at the table." At first, I thought it was more of a challenge, but without even thinking to answer back or challenge him, I just found myself removing my cap. Neville then explained that it was bad manners to wear a hat at the table while eating, and that it was bad manners to wear one inside the house at all. I didn't laugh out loud, but inside I was chuckling, thinking to myself, who made up those rules?

The food came out, and it was beautiful: chicken, rice, and mutton. Usually, I would pick up the chicken in my hands, but I was trying to be perceived as someone with manners, so I started to cut it off the bone. A smirk came across Neville's face, and he said, "Pick it up." When I hesitated, he said it again. "You pick up your chicken." He himself was eating his chicken off the bone. "You don't need to use your knife and fork to eat chicken. You can pick it up." And so, I did. It was almost as if he knew that I was nervous about it.

Eunice joined us at the table, and they started asking me about my interests, what I liked to do, and what life was like in the children's home. I told them I enjoyed playing football and listening to loud music. I asked them what they got up to, and Neville said he liked playing dominoes and cards and meeting his friends at the pub. Eunice said she went to church in Nechells and followed the Lord; that was her faith. It was an interesting conversation; one I hadn't really had with people before. After we finished dinner, we sat and watched TV for a while, and then they brought me back to St Athan's Croft. Dino asked me how things had gone and whether I'd like to go again. I said it was an interesting visit, and I thought they seemed like nice people.

I had one more visit after school, and then it was time for my first stopover. I remember sleeping in that bed for the first night, and it was the most comfortable, relaxing sleep I'd had in a long time. No springy mattress; no loud noises at night from other young boys who couldn't get to sleep or were struggling with nightmares; no night-waker turning the lights on; no sound of the local gang walking past the home singing, "Where's your Mama gone?" and throwing stones at the plastic windows. Just bliss, calm, and a sense of tranquillity.

In the morning, Eunice came in with a cup of tea. She asked if I'd had a good night's sleep and whether this was somewhere I could call home. I remember stretching out my arms and saying, "Yes, I think I could."

And so, the process of moving from St Athan's Croft to Witton Lodge Road to live with Eunice and Neville began. It was a familiar path I was used to: the road of trust. A road that had become fragile and broken. A road with lots of bumps, an unsmooth road with tough terrain, ready to be walked down again for the tenth time. This was my tenth foster home. Why will it not break like the last nine? Why do I suddenly have this unknown faith in a place, a home, and a people that seemed okay on the outside but might not be so on the inside? Why this one? Why now? Why don't I just age out of care in this children's home? And yet, I find myself leaving.

In 1999, mobile phones were just starting to become cool, but cool because all you could do was play Snake, text, and phone. I suppose that's when a mobile phone was a mobile phone. My first phone was a Nokia 402, and phones were forbidden in the home. If you were caught with one, it would be confiscated, and you wouldn't get it back until the day you left. The only thing we were allowed was a pager. I remember the manager, Lloyd, was very strict about mobile phones.

There seemed to be some sort of mix-up with me leaving because Lloyd had said I wasn't leaving for two weeks, but my social worker said it would be by the end of the week. Like an idiot, after doing so well to hide my Nokia 402, one morning Lloyd came in to wake me up. I woke up with hazy eyes to him grinning at the end of my bed with my phone in his hand. "Ah," he said, "another one for the collection." I was upset and angry, but then I realised I was going in two days anyway, so he'd have to give it back. I told him, "You've only got it in your collection for two days, and then you'll be giving it back to me."

He said, "More like two weeks."

I said, "We'll see."

"Okay, we'll see," he replied.

Because he was the manager of the home, I just assumed he knew more than I did. Anyway, it turned out it was actually two days, not two weeks. You should have seen the look on Lloyd's face when he handed me my phone back. I said to him, "Looks like it was only a two-day collection, Lloyd." He smiled, put his hand on my shoulder, and handed me my phone back. "Look after yourself, young man," he said. "Go and make this work."

And so, I left St Athan's croft children's home for the last time. I left children's homes for the last time. And this was the last time I would move around the care system because I was about to go and live with Eunice and Neville, two of the greatest people I've ever known. One of the biggest things I admire about them is their ability to remain structured and with firm boundaries. Their level of teamwork was excellent. There was no chance to play one off the other; there was no room for me to manipulate. They were tight as water, their communication was on point, and although I tried every opportunity, I figured out pretty quickly that that just wasn't going to slide with them.

Of course, I brought some bad habits from the children's home, like smoking weed. A couple of the boys who lived around the area and went to my school also smoked, and one of them was a guy called Matthew. Matthew was a couple of years older than me, and he smoked a lot of weed. Before I knew it, I was out there smoking cannabis too. Looking back, this was probably my way of testing the boundaries with Eunice and Neville.

They were aware of Matthew, but they didn't know too much about him. They just knew he probably wasn't going to be the greatest influence on me, and they tried to warn me about that. This came after I'd brought Matthew back to the house a few times and introduced him. Matthew wasn't a bad lad—he wasn't rude, he was well-mannered, and he was a nice young man—but he smoked a lot of cannabis, and I got involved in that.

One day, I came back to the house after what we used to call a "session" of chilling in the park, smoking weed. I had my hat pulled down, covering most of my eyes. Neville answered the door and asked me where I'd been. I said, "I've just been out with Matthew." He looked at me and said, "You've been smoking weed, haven't you?" I quickly replied, "No." He asked, "Then why are your eyes so red?" I said, "I must have hay fever." He laughed and said, "Don't be silly. I'm not stupid. You need to cut that stupidness out, and don't be coming back here under the influence of cannabis again. You understand?"

Around that time, I started dating a girl in the local area called Alexis. Alexis was beautiful, and her parents were also part of the church. Eunice knew Alexis's mom, who went to the same church, so they were happy I'd found someone who was a positive influence on me. You could say Alexis was my first proper girlfriend, although there were many more to come over the next few years.

I'd been dating Alexis for some time, but I was still hanging around with Matthew, chilling and smoking weed. One day, I came back to the house, and Neville opened the door. He asked me where I'd been, and I immediately said, "I've been with Alexis," because I didn't want him to know I'd been with Matthew. He looked at me and said, "You've been with Matthew, haven't you? I can smell the weed on you, and I can see your eyes are red." I doubled down and said, "No, Nev, I've been with Alexis. I promise."

Now, picture Neville standing half in and half out of the door. I couldn't see into the house. He said, "I'll give you the option to tell me the truth. If you're lying, you'll be grounded for a week. Where have you been, and who have you been with?" I stuck to my story: "I've been at the park with Alexis."

Neville gave me that disappointed look, and without saying a word, he opened the door fully. That's when I saw through to the lounge—and there was Alexis, sitting on the couch with a confused look on her face. I had no words. The blood drained from my face. Neville asked Alexis to leave because I was grounded.

I couldn't believe I'd been caught red-handed, but it turned out to be such a valuable life lesson. The thought of being in that situation again was so embarrassing that I've always aimed to be honest with people where I can. I aim to be real about things.

The beauty of Eunice and Neville was that no matter my behaviour, no matter my reaction, they always met me with understanding, love, and discipline that made sense to me. I always knew where the line was. They never moved the goalposts to confuse me; they stayed true to their principles and values. They would say, "You are loved, but sometimes we need to tell you where the boundary is. And when you cross it, we will let you know. It's not personal, but we are here to prepare you for the world. We are here to prepare you for adult life."

Those small seeds of belonging they had planted from the moment they walked through St Athan's doors were starting to bud. That sense of belonging was beginning to feel very real. Maybe this was actually going to work. Or maybe it was just false hope knocking on the door again—who knows? But there was something trustworthy about them, something that made me want to believe.

I must admit, I wasn't a big fan of going to prayer meetings with Eunice every Thursday evening. Because of the whole weed thing, I wasn't trusted to stay in the house alone, so I had to go with her. Every Thursday, we'd cram into this small room with about 20 people, all praying to God and singing songs. As you can imagine, it was the most boring time. These meetings dragged on from 6 p.m. to 9 p.m., singing to the Lord. The only fun I found in those dismal three hours was banging the tambourine, but apart from that, it was mind-numbing.

One time, I was so bored I decided to join in with the song they were singing. I still remember it to this day, like it's been engraved in my memory: "Jesus, build a fence around me every day." Eunice didn't know I was singing out of pure boredom; she thought I was having a great time. That evening, she came back excited to tell Neville that I'd been touched by the Lord. I made a joke, saying, "The Lord hasn't touched me at all—that would be completely wrong."

Every other Sunday, I had to go to church. This wasn't by choice. I found Sunday school so boring, although some of the church girls were pretty hot, and we did have some interesting conversations about respecting your body, sex before marriage, and all that. Again, it wasn't where I wanted to be on a Sunday morning, but I suppose it gave me a sense of something different—something inherently good, something unknown yet peaceful. In hindsight, being bored on a Sunday morning was still healthier than being stoned in a park.

What I do know is that change is gradual. That's why I always come back to the idea of drip by drip, day by day. Nothing happens overnight. It's all gradual, it's all repetition, it's all arduous and mundane, and it's not without challenge.

I used to absolutely love the "Rubber Special." Hold on a minute—let me explain. Neville's nickname, known by family and friends, was Rubber. It had nothing to do with condoms; it was because he worked at Fort Dunlop, in a factory making plane tyres.

He once told me a story about unconscious racism—although, when he told me, it seemed pretty conscious to me. His boss kept a picture of Neville and a few other workers in a frame on his mantelpiece in the office. One day, Neville went in to speak to him about something, and his boss, in a humorous and jovial way, said he'd been teaching his kid about fire safety over the weekend. He told his kid, "If you go near the fire, you'll end up like those guys in the picture," alluding to the photo of Neville and his teammates because they were Black.

Neville said he felt angry in the moment but didn't express it out of fear of losing his job. He simply left the office. Later, he told me, "Sometimes in life, you want to show people how angry you are. You might even want to punch someone in the face. But we must rise above it. We can't allow those people to see us affected by their negligence. Sometimes, Steven, your biggest power is in your smile and walking away."

That stuck with me. It wasn't just a lesson about racism; it was a lesson about life.

Anyway, back to the Rubber Special. When Neville came back from the pub, he was the happiest person in the world—a man filled with love. All he wanted to do was feed everyone, and so he'd make us his famous Rubber Special. It involved eggs, bacon, sausage, beans, mushrooms, and some special seasoning. It was so good. Essentially, it was an English breakfast, but we never called it that—it was always the Rubber Special.

Afterwards, we'd sit in the back room and have a cigarette. Now, I know exactly what you're thinking: How irresponsible of Neville to condone smoking with a 15-year-old. Well, it wasn't just me. There were a few children who came to live with us. The first was a lad called Malcolm. Interestingly, Malcolm's brother used to live with me in St Athan's, so I already knew of him. Malcolm was a cool kid, and we'd chill with Neville and have a cheeky cigarette.

Eunice hated it. She hated the smell and would tell Neville off, but it was his way of connecting with us on a different level. He would never supply us with cigarettes, but he used it as a window to connect with us, to listen to us, to mentor us. To be quite honest, some of my greatest memories with Neville were those days—or the trips in his Jeep, playing old reggae tunes. He absolutely loved that, Jeep.

By this point in the story, I had been living with Eunice and Neville for two years. I was 15 years old, just starting Year 11, and I remember September 11th, 2001, like it was yesterday. I came in from school, and Neville was sitting in his armchair, staring at the TV screen with a shocked look on his face. My first thought was that it was a movie. They were playing clips of planes flying into buildings, and then the news reporter came on to say two planes had flown into the World Trade Centre buildings in New York, America.

The most haunting part was watching people jump to their deaths out of the buildings. I mean, what a choice for a person to make—knowing you're going to die and having to quickly decide which option: burn to death or jump to your death. And here's me, complaining to Eunice about what's for dinner because I'm so used to eating Caribbean meals, and on this particular evening, I'm eating basic bangers and mash.

That experience put life into perspective. It made me realise how small my complaints were in the grand scheme of things. Then Neville hit me with a great line: "Steven, life is short, so you have to live the life you love and love the life you live." I think he may have got it from a song, but it's a quote I've never forgotten.

Not all lessons came from serious moments, though. I remember one night Neville became so angry with me that he told me to go to my room. We'd just finished watching an old-school movie called Dracula, and the main actor was Peter Cushing. But when the credits came up at the end, the font was in old English, and the "C" in Cushion looked like a "G." So I said, "The actor's name is Peter Gushion."

Neville looked at me with a puzzled expression and said, "His name is Peter Cushion, not Gushion."

I wasn't having it. "No, it's not. That was definitely Gushion."

Unfortunately, we couldn't rewind it, but I could feel Neville getting increasingly agitated by my insistence. He raised his voice and said, "His name is Peter Cushion, not Gushion!"

Now, I should have left it there. But I was like a dog with a bone. "No, Nev, it was definitely a G."

His eyes glazed over, and I swear I could see metaphorical steam coming out of his ears. He stood up over me and said, "Go to your bed, you rude boy. Go to your damn bed!"

So, I went to bed with a cheeky smirk on my face.

The lesson here? Sometimes, you just have to accept what someone is saying as their truth. And to this very day, guess what Neville calls me when we meet? With a big, wide smile on his face, he calls me, "Gushion."

Jamaica

One of my greatest memories with Eunice and Neville was Jamaica. In 2002, I stepped on a plane for the first time in my life, ready to embark on a nine-hour flight via Air Jamaica, bound for Montego Bay. Jamaica—the home of both Eunice and Neville's families. It was, quite simply, the trip of a lifetime and a real honour to visit Eunice and Neville's original home.

We stayed with Eunice's mother and father in St Ann's Bay, which is where Bob Marley was from. We arrived in the early hours, and I still remember that hot air rushing through the plane as soon as the doors opened. It was such a surreal moment. Then came the taxi drive into St Ann's Bay. There was no Sandals resort for us. In fact, we drove past a Sandals resort, and Neville laughed, saying, "They might get the Jamaican weather, but they don't get the real Jamaican culture."

When we arrived at Eunice's parents' house, it was beautiful, even in the middle of the night. I woke up the next morning to the sound of barking dogs. "Come, Steven, it's breakfast time." I was officially in paradise. I looked out the window, and the sky was a bright blue—not a cloud in sight. The house was more like a bungalow, as there were no stairs.

I stepped out onto the veranda and was met by Eunice's mum and dad. They welcomed me with open arms and gave me a big hug. For breakfast, it was eggs, bacon, bread, and orange juice. It tasted so good.

As I looked around outside, there was a real sense of community. Neighbours were talking to each other, and I even saw one guy cutting boys' hair on his lawn. He asked me if I wanted a haircut, but I said no because I'd already had mine done. Then he asked if I had a sister. I said no and asked why. He said, "You've got good skin and nice eyes, so if you have a sister, I know she would look pretty."

I will never forget my experience of Jamaica—it was quite simply incredible.

We went to visit Neville's family in St Elizabeth. They didn't have much. Their home was like a shack in the sticks, with little room. I remember having to share a bed with Eunice and Neville. One night, there was a reggae festival, and Neville, his cousins, and I went. We danced all night, and I drank Red Stripe, the beer of Jamaica. It was pure paradise.

Here I was, this care kid who thought he'd given up on his sense of belonging, and yet here I was in Jamaica with two people who only saw Steven. Not my behaviour, not my circumstance, not this half-caste kid with no identity. They saw me as worthy. They wanted me to feel what it was like to be in a family. They gave me a sense of purpose and experiences I would never have had without giving it a go.

There was one scary moment for me in Jamaica. Eunice's mum's neighbour decided to take me into Kingston, the capital. I was up for anything—I wanted to see as much of Jamaica as possible. We ended up in this voodoo shop that looked like an old-style American bar, the kind with two swinging doors. Inside, there were potions, soaps, elixirs, and remedies.

The lady I was with said, "Stay here. I'm just going to a shop, and I'll be back."

I'm telling you; I sat in that voodoo shop for well over an hour, just staring at potions and herbs. I began to get worried. I had no phone, I didn't know where I was, and this lady hadn't returned. I decided to look outside the shop to see if I could spot her, but all I saw was a busy market and a lot of foreign, scary faces looking back at me. So, I went back into the shop and waited.

Eventually, she came back and apologised for her lateness. I tried to play it off as no big deal, but inside, I was raging. She bought me a KFC to make up for it and let me tell you—there's something about Jamaican KFC. It was so, so good.

After seeing Neville's family in St Elizabeth, we went to see more of Eunice's family in a place called Black River. It was one of the most memorable moments of the trip. Their house was on the beach—literally, their back garden was the beach. I'm talking white sand, palm trees, and see-through sea. It was like I'd jumped into a page from a holiday magazine.

The reason it was so memorable was because the family had gone out on their boat, caught a live lobster, cooked it on a BBQ, and seasoned it. So here I was, this care kid from inner-city Birmingham, lying on a deck chair in paradise, eating BBQ lobster with a can of Red Stripe in my right hand and the warm Jamaican breeze on my face.

I looked over at Eunice and Neville, smiling at me, and in that moment, it was as if time had stopped. It was as if the universe had put her arms around me and said, "I told you everything would be okay."

That's why I absolutely love the Bob Marley song Three Little Birds. It reminds little Steven that despite the pain, despite the rejection, he too would find his purpose. He too was worthy of love. And he too would find a sense of belonging.

Eunice and Neville, Molly, and Rubber—these are two of the most impactful pairs of people in my childhood.

First came Pat, my first experience of a mother. Then came Dave. When my forever family broke down, he was there in my first children's home to remind me that I wasn't a problem, that I wasn't damaged goods. Later in life, we reconnected and embarked on an incredible journey together.

Then there was Adam, the only child I could trust. He gave me the feeling of companionship and brotherhood when I needed it most.

And finally, there was Eunice and Neville—my last hope in family, my last hope in people, my last hope in belonging. And boy, did they deliver.

I'm not lucky to have met these incredible people along the way—I am blessed.

So, what's the one word that connects these five awesome human beings? What's the one thing I think about when I think of them? And what's the one thing that feels right when I say their names?

You got it: belonging.

I belonged with them, and I belonged to them. I was their son, I was their friend, I was their family. Not Steven the care kid. Not Steven the naughty kid. Not Steven the half-caste kid. Just Steven.

A kid searching for belonging.

And they were there for me.

I found my people. My tribe. My family.

Drip By Drip Day By Day

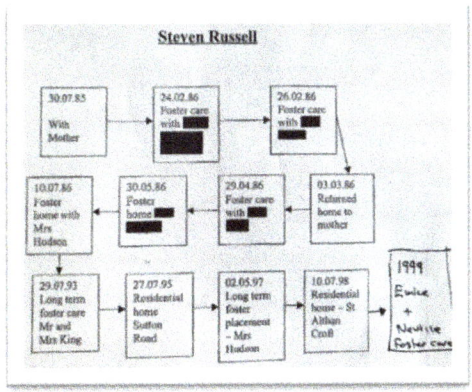

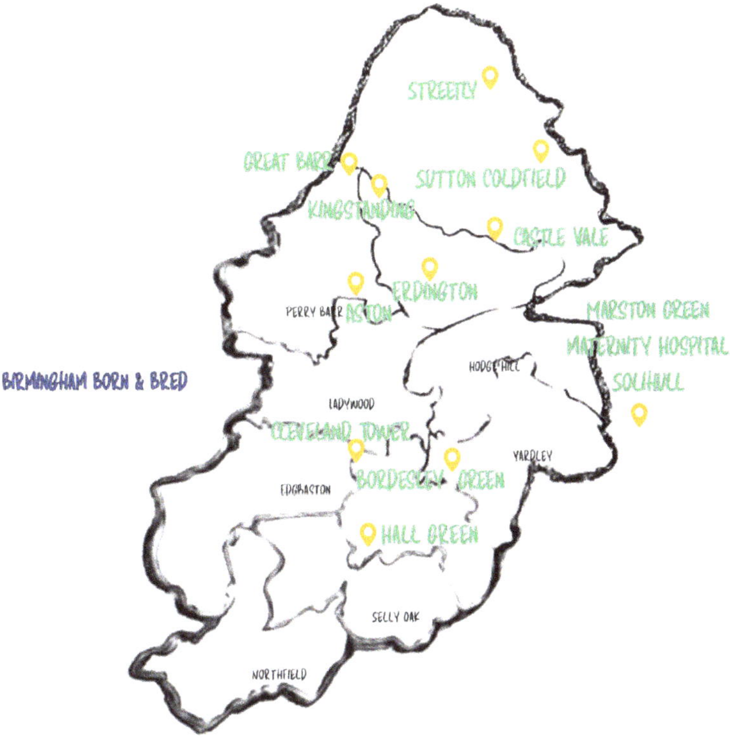

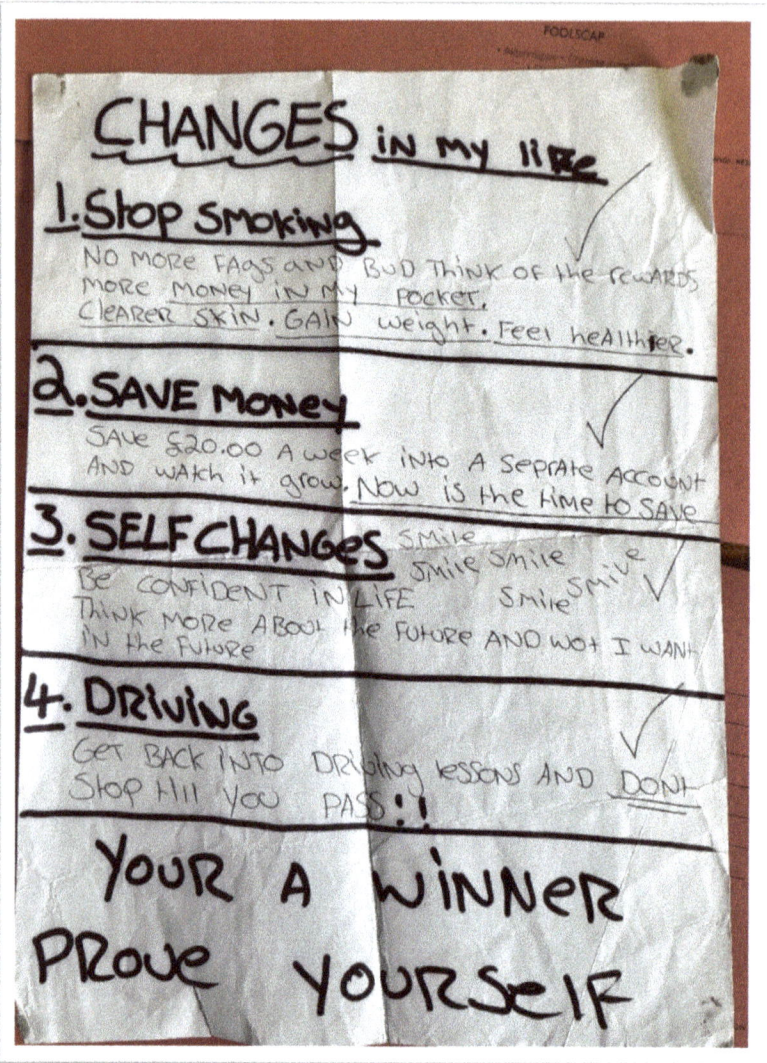

Eleven

I'm Not a Care Leaver

For those unfamiliar with the language of the care system—amongst the LACs (Looked After Children), PEPs (Personal Education Plans), CICs (Children in Care), and CINs (Children in Need)—there lies another term: Care Leaver. It's a systemic label, a bureaucratic stamp used to describe a young person who is no longer under the local authority's formal care. But when you break down the true meaning of 'care' and 'leaver', you quickly see how flawed and cold this term really is. Yet somehow, as a society, we've grown comfortable with labelling young people in this way. So, without getting lost in the semantics, the real question is: are they leaving the system, or are they leaving the care?

Let me ask you: what does care mean to you? And what does leaver mean to you? The word 'leaver', when it comes to children, reminds me of those Year 6 hoodies they get when leaving primary school. You know the ones—embroidered with '2025 Leavers' in bold on the back, surrounded by the names of all their classmates. It's a fun way to mark the end of an era before they move on to secondary school. But would you call them 'education leavers? Of course not. They're simply moving on to their next chapter. Even when they finish secondary school in Year 11, they might be called 'school leavers', but no one refers to them as 'education leavers. Why? Because we all understand that education is lifelong.

And that's my point. Despite leaving the system they've lived in, a young person's right to be cared for should also be lifelong. Labelling them as 'care leavers' is, in itself, not very caring. It suggests an abrupt end, a final departure from support and connection. Think about it: when your child turns 18, would you call them a care leaver? Even if they move out one day (if they can afford to, of course), would you ever label them that way? The thought is absurd. You don't stop caring just because they've reached a certain age or live at a different address. And yet, for young people in the system, there's a constant, formal reminder that they are different from their peers. It's system-led, not care-led.

This label is the final insult to an emotional injury that has been inflicted over many years. From needing risk assessments just to stay at a friend's house overnight, to being singled out as a 'LAC kid' in school and attending PEP meetings, there's a persistent voice that says: You are different. You can't be normal because the system doesn't allow you to be. This label chips away at a young person's self-esteem. It can make them feel disposable, as if the care they received had an expiration date. It affects their opportunities, their relationships, and how they see their place in the world. And so, the final label that's supposed to stick forever is: I am a care leaver.

Well, I don't identify as a care leaver. I have no judgement for those who do—many have bravely taken ownership of the term, and that is their right and their choice. But for me, it's a systemic label that has no relevance to my identity or my journey. One of the greatest reasons I don't identify as a care leaver is because I was still being cared for by my foster parents, Eunice and Neville, long after I left their home. Every Sunday, I'd go back for dinner and sit with Neville to watch football. How could I be a care leaver when the care never left?

The Dawn of Adulthood

The system's plan for my transition to adulthood was decided in a meeting between my social worker, Eunice, and Neville. I would go and live with their son, Chris—my foster brother—in Aston, on Village Road, right next to the Aston Villa football ground. Naturally, because this was all very new, there was a sense of excitement.

College hadn't worked out for me. I had been studying leisure and tourism, which was one of those subjects that kids without GCSE passes often ended up doing. I had to choose between science and leisure and tourism, and at the time, the latter felt like the better option. However, it only lasted a couple of months before I stopped going, at which point, Eunice told me I needed to find work.

So, before I officially moved out, I started working at a local warehouse, just a five-minute walk from my new home in Aston. The company was called William Gosling and Sons, a corrugated factory that produced cardboard boxes for companies like Bristan and Armitage Shanks, bathroom manufacturers.

I had spent the previous week looking for work without any luck. One day, as I was walking past the warehouse, I noticed some guys outside and asked if there were any jobs going. The first response was no, but then Carl, the manager, asked what kind of work I was looking for. I told him, "Anything," and he said, "Yeah."

I remember starting off at £3.50 an hour, sweeping the warehouse floors. It felt liberating. For me, it was about building my work ethic, something no one had ever really taught me. I ended up staying at William Gosling and Sons for a while, and by that point, I was also living in Aston. Getting to and from work was easy—I had a bike that I used to cycle to work and to Eunice and Nevilles for dinner.

Living on my own was a steep learning curve. The system had prepared me with a 'leaving care grant'—a small sum of money to buy essentials—but it hadn't prepared me for the reality of budgeting, cooking, or managing a home. I was developing my work ethic while fumbling through how to live independently. The great thing for me was that I still had Eunice and Neville. Even though I was getting involved in silly behaviours—like smoking cannabis, hanging around with people who didn't have my best interests at heart (some of them local gang members), bringing girls back, and letting the kitchen bin overflow with folded pizza boxes—I always knew Eunice and Neville were there.

My financial routine was non-existent, and I wasn't eating healthily. The only time I ate properly was when I went to Eunice and Neville's every Sunday. That was the embodiment of being cared for—knowing that they were always just a phone call away, that their door was always open. Again, this went against the term 'care leaver', because the care was always there, filling the gaps the system had left behind.

Even now, as a 39-year-old man writing this book, I can still pick up the phone and go to see them. The care never stopped. I was stumbling my way through adulthood, not really knowing what it meant. But there I was, living with my foster brother in Aston, cycling to work every day. Things could have been a lot worse.

At work, I progressed from sweeping floors to operating some of the machinery. Eventually, I was asked if I'd like to learn how to drive a forklift truck. I began lessons on operating a counterbalance forklift truck and earned my licence.

One day, while I was sweeping the floor as usual, an older man in the warehouse, called Cookie, approached me. He had been there for many years—a humble, wise soul with a calm nature. He was also very good at table tennis.

Cookie said to me, "You know, Steve, you can tell a lot about a person by the way they sweep the floor."

I asked, "What do you mean?"

He explained, "Some people sweep the floor and push all the rubbish into the corner of the room, prop the broomstick against the wall, and walk away. These people don't like to finish jobs. They don't complete tasks and rely on others to do it for them—there's an air of laziness about them.

"Then there are others who sweep around objects. They won't move pallets, tables, or chairs to clean properly; they just sweep around them. Again, it shows a lack of willingness to get the job done properly—a lack of completion, just like the first group.

"But then there are people like you. I've watched you sweep the floor many times. You move the pallets, clear the corners, and even sweep under the racks to get the cobwebs. You sweep everything into the middle of the room, and I've even seen you on your hands and knees sweeping up the tiny fragments. That's a strong work ethic. It shows someone who wants to do their absolute best with what they've got. No cutting corners, no expecting others to finish the job for them. True clarity and commitment to doing their best."

At the time, as a 16-year-old sweeping floors, I didn't fully grasp the message. But now, I understand. Cookie was talking about work ethic. He was planting a seed of self-worth. That work ethic is still within me today. Whether I'm sweeping floors or offering emotional support to a dysregulated child, the mindset remains the same: How can I get the very best out of this situation? How can I make the most of what I've got to work with?

Between 2002 and 2006, the main people in my life were Matthew, Tommy, and Dave. Matthew was a friend I'd known since living with Eunice and Neville. Although they didn't approve of him—mainly because of his heavy cannabis use—he was someone I liked. Tommy, my cousin, lived in South Birmingham. I'd known him my whole life, and he was basically a brother to me. And then, of course, there was Dave. Dave was always there, a steady guide.

It didn't take long for me to realise that I was no longer under the confinement—or comfort—of the adults around me. One day, Chris told me he was moving in with his girlfriend. He said he'd check on me, but the responsibility of the house was now mine. At the time, I was dating a girl called Jessica, so I had some company. But there was still this lingering sense of being alone, a feeling I'd always carried. Even though I was about to turn 18, I still had no real understanding of aspirations or direction.

I used to say to Dave, "I just want to have some purpose, some meaning." But with no clear idea of what that was, I'd resort to the same old habits: cannabis, late nights, empty pizza boxes. I suppose it was all part of me trying to figure things out. The thing I loved most about Dave was that he never pressured me. He'd just say, "Keep the determination. Keep striving. Keep searching. Eventually, you'll find what you're looking for."

By the time I was 19, I was working at a different company, Anixter UK. I'd been driving a forklift for a year and moved because it paid more. I even had a Warehouse Distribution Level 2 certificate. One weekend, I decided to throw a party with my mate Pete, who I'd lived with at St Athans Croft Children's Home. The party was lively—music, drinking, smoking.

At one point, I went into the front room and noticed two girls arguing. Before I knew it, one was pulling the other's hair. I stepped in to break it up, but then one of the girls' boyfriends attacked me. Suddenly, there was a full-blown street fight outside.

I remember feeling something hit my head. My first thought was that someone had thrown a drink at me because I felt a wet sensation running down my neck. But when I touched the back of my head, I realised it wasn't beer—it was blood. My right index finger sank into a wound. That's when I realised, I'd been stabbed. I dropped to the ground. My cousin Tommy was slapping my face, telling me not to close my eyes. At that moment, I felt a strange sense of warmth, a feeling that I was about to die.

The police arrived, and I remember suddenly standing up, shouting in fear. I was taken to Queen Elizabeth Hospital, where my head was patched up with glue. The nurse told me I was lucky to be alive.

Dave came to collect me. For the first time, I saw deep disappointment in his eyes. He looked at me and said, "Steve, I could have been seeing you in a morgue this morning. I don't know how much more I've got to give." When Dave dropped me back, I remember seeing the bloodstains on the floor. I grabbed the first piece of paper I could find—a utility bill—and on the blank side, I wrote a list:

- Stop smoking weed
- Stop drinking
- Move out of Aston
- Get a new number
- Start working
- Start driving
- Talk to people with respect
- Smile more
- Be more confident

Between 2005 and 2006, I achieved everything on that list. It was then I realised that everything I ever needed—every resource, every tool, every ounce of power—was already inside me. It just took someone like Dave to see it in me when so many others couldn't.

So now it's 2005. I'm 20 years old. It's been a year since I was stabbed. I'm living in a flat in, about to apply for a position in a children's home. I'm regularly seeing Eunice, Neville, and Dave. I'm working two jobs. I've just passed my driving test, and I'm ready to begin.

Then Dave asks if I'd like to go to New York with him. He handmakes miniature bears and is making the trip to sell them. I'd always wanted to go to America. We flew from Birmingham to Amsterdam, then from Schiphol Airport to New York. About three hours into the flight, the captain announced there was trouble with one of the jets. The decision was made to turn back. As the tension on the plane grew, Dave, being Dave, decided to walk around, praying for people who were visibly upset. I was mortified, sinking into my seat. But that was Dave—he didn't care what anyone thought. He just wanted to help.

New York was incredible. The life, the energy—it was everything I'd imagined. We went to Times Square, Brooklyn, Queens, and the memorial site of 9/11. But it wasn't just a holiday. Dave used the trip to solidify his mentoring. One day, as we walked through the city, he said, "You could be on a plane like this, travelling the world for your own business." His words stayed with me.

While we were in New York, Dave got a call to say his sister had passed away. It was devastating, and for the first time, I felt it was my turn to be there for him. Before we left, Dave had said, "This trip will either make us or break us." There's no doubt—it made us.

Over the years, I travelled with Dave to Chicago and Germany, each trip was an incredible adventure with the most incredible person. Dave was, and still is, the greatest human I've ever known.

This chapter of my life wasn't about leaving care. I was never a care leaver. I was a young person navigating a chaotic system, yes, but I was never without care. People like Pat, Adam, Eunice, Neville, Cookie, and Dave were constant reminders of humanity, compassion, and the fact that I mattered.

My journey highlights a universal truth: we all need connection to thrive. Care isn't a service to be switched off; it's a fundamental human need. It's the mentor who sees potential, the foster parent whose door is always open, the colleague who offers quiet wisdom or the friend who always has your back. My work ethic grew not in a vacuum, but because Cookie took the time to notice me. My identity was forged not by a label, but by the belief Dave had in me. My resilience was built on the foundation of care that Eunice and Neville provided, a safety net the system could never offer.

Yes, I experienced moments where I didn't feel cared for, but I never saw myself as someone leaving care. The care never left me. It was always there, staring me in the face.

So, I don't identify as a care leaver. I identify as someone who knows struggle. Someone who has faced emotional and physical pain. Someone who was lost, isolated, and rejected—but overcame. I identify as someone who has risen, who has found the power within.

And all of that stems from the people who continued to care for me.

I'm not a care leaver. I am cared for.

Twelve

Torn

This, by far, is the most difficult chapter to write. It's a chapter I wrote during a period of feeling torn from the family I had spent my entire life searching for. I'm also keenly aware that, for some of you, it may be difficult to accept my decision to leave—perhaps because of your own internal biases, a potential discomfort around family breakdowns, or simply because you have your own views and opinions on what family should be. All of this is perfectly fine and normal. If we were to sit down in a coffee shop and discuss this chapter, there would be no judgement on your views or opinions. I can only tell this story as it is—from my heart and my mind. It doesn't make it right or wrong; it just makes it honest and true from my perspective.

Take a moment to imagine yourself standing in the middle of a triangle. Surrounding you are three points. At one point, you see three humans—three little humans who are your children. One is 14, one is 13, and one is 11. You're about to deliver some news that will change and alter the course of their lives, knowing full well they have no control over the news you're about to deliver or the action you're about to take.

Then you turn to the second point of the triangle, and you see everything you've built over the past 15 years: your home, your family, your community, your neighbours, your job, your hobbies, your friends. An address you've called home for 13 years. All of it is about to come to an end.

Finally, you turn to the last point of the triangle, and staring back at you is your younger self. Your child self. And they're asking, "Why? Why are you doing this? Isn't this what you've always wanted? Isn't this everything we've strived for? All you've ever wanted was your own family. You've lived with 10 foster families, two children's homes, you've had to make and break friends over five schools, with multiple adults and multiple places. Finally, you've found and created your own family. So why are we not enough? Have we not been enough?"

All of these questions, coming from the child I once was.

And so, you stand in the middle of this triangle, and you feel torn. You feel broken. You feel like a failure—pulled apart by the weight of your choices.

The day I looked into my children's eyes to tell them I was ending the relationship with their mum (Laura) was a dark day for me.

It felt as though I was stealing something special from them, taking that which is sacred to them, and I was removing this from their lives, knowing they had no choice but to accept my decision.

Laura and I called all three children to the dinner table to tell them the news as they ate their pizza. Alyssa was excitable; she wanted to know what the suspense was all about, so I said, "Me and your mum have something important to tell you." Within an instant, Alyssa said, "Are you breaking up?" I had planned to pull the plaster off slowly and explain it had been extremely tough for both their mum and me. However, Alyssa, in that breath, gave me permission to pull the plaster off quickly.

"Yes, we have decided to bring our relationship to an end. However, we will do what is called 'co-parenting,' meaning we don't stop being your mum and dad, and we will work hard together to ensure all your needs are being met."

I looked over towards Malachi, our eldest child of 14, and noticed an expression on his face I had not seen before. I noticed his eyes had glazed over as he looked back at me. It felt like I could see the speech bubbles popping out of his head saying, "Why are you leaving me?", "Please don't go?", "Why are you doing this?"

The 14-year-old hormonal teenager couldn't bring himself to physical words. Instead, he slumped himself into his chair, putting down that now cold slice of pizza, attempting to wear his brave, masculine face. I couldn't help but see the 2-year-old Malachi, the 8-year-old Malachi looking back at me. It was probably the most difficult part of this experience, knowing I had caused them pain, knowing this was something I never wanted them or me to experience.

Cory (13) was sitting on my left-hand side. I have always seen a part of little Steven inside of Cory, which I suppose means there is a closeness between Cory and me that is undeniable. Cory is a beautiful soul, full of creativity, vibrancy, love, and tenacity.

As parents, we often say we love all our children the same way. However, although our ultimate love for them may be on the same wavelength, the way in which we love our children can be completely different because they are different to each other. I have a special relationship with all my children, which is something I have always and will always treasure. Malachi is my firstborn, so I have loved him for longer, and no child came before him; he will always be so special to me because of this, and watching him grow into the kind, protective, and strong young man he is now has been a privilege and an honour.

Alyssa is my only daughter, and she is my youngest child. I have always felt a strong sense of protection towards Alyssa. I have always been affectionate towards her, ensuring she has never missed a hug or a kiss before she goes to sleep or before she leaves for school.

From as far back as I can remember, Cory and I have always had a close, loving, humorous relationship, with him always being such a happy, laughing, bouncy child. He reminded me so much of myself as a child. Our connection is strong, and he will often seek me out, wanting to be close to me.

So now I'm looking towards my child, after being told his dad is leaving the family home, with his head on the table over his hands, with no words. He manages 2–3 minutes before leaving to go to his bedroom. I go to console him, but his mum says to give him some time by himself. Then, Malachi and Alyssa begin the onslaught of questions to see what they can salvage from this emotional bomb site.

"Where are you going to live?"

"Will we have two birthdays?"

"When are you leaving?"

"When will we see you?"

Outwardly, they were being curious, inquisitive, smiling, and chatty.

Inwardly, you could see the pain, the uncertainty, the disappointment, and the hurt.

There was no reassuring them things would be okay, there was no inspirational message, just two parents sat at the table with their children, attempting to pick up the pieces from something that had been shattered all over the floor.

And then there was Laura.

I hadn't truly looked at her during that conversation with the children—not until the questions had subsided and the room fell into a heavy silence. When I finally turned to her, I saw a woman who had given everything to this relationship, to me, to our family. She sat there, hands clasped over her mouth in a prayer-like gesture, her eyes brimming with tears she refused to let fall.

Laura had always been the calm in my storm, the steady hand when I faltered. She had loved me in ways I didn't know how to love myself, filling the gaps I left behind with her patience, her kindness, and her unwavering belief in me. And yet, in that moment, I could see the weight of 16 years pressing down on her—the heartbreak of watching the life we'd built together unravel before her eyes.

She didn't say much that evening. She didn't need to. Her silence spoke volumes. It wasn't anger or bitterness; it was grief. Grief for the family we had created, for the dreams we had shared, and for the man she had stood by, even when he couldn't fully stand by her.

Laura had always been the better half of us. She was the one who held everything together when I couldn't. And now, as I prepared to leave, I knew I was asking her to carry a burden she didn't deserve. She would have to pick up the pieces, to be the constant for our children while I figured out how to be the father they needed.

I don't think I'll ever be able to fully articulate the gratitude I feel for Laura. She is, and always will be, one of the most incredible people I've ever known. She gave me a family when I didn't know how to have one. She gave me love when I didn't know how to receive it. And even in the end, when I made the decision to leave, she gave me grace.

Laura didn't deserve the pain I caused her, but she bore it with a strength that I will always admire. She is the kind of person who makes the world a better place simply by being in it. And though our paths have diverged, I will forever be grateful for the years we shared and the family we created together.

How did we get to here, you may be wondering? Well, let's go back to 2007, where I first met Laura, this innocent, humble, beautiful human being.

I was 22 years of age at the time and had been working at DHL (a logistical company) as a forklift truck driver. I aspired to do something with meaning and to become someone with purpose. I just felt my life was destined for more than driving a forklift truck every night.

So, I'm on my break, sat on the forklift truck drinking my machine-made hot chocolate, reading the newspaper, and I see an advertisement to become a residential support worker in a children's home. I spoke with Dave about the opportunity (as my mentor), and he helped me to prepare for an interview, and I ended up getting the job. So, of course, I handed in my notice to DHL and prepared to leave after 31 days.

One of the days, I was working the belt. When packages came down the belt, it was my job to read the code and then put the package in the right cage. I looked to my left and saw this new girl, and I began speaking to her and found out her name was Laura. I would crack jokes, be rebellious and cheeky, and she seemed to like my humour. Laura was studying to be a nurse at university but wanted to take the opportunity to earn some extra money, so she put university to the side to explore a better income. It was her sister, Sam, who informed her about the opportunity at DHL, and her mum was a manager there too. So, we spoke some more over the coming weeks, and eventually, we began to date.

It's important to state at this stage of my life, my mindset around girls hadn't changed since I was 15. I was highly immature and only saw girls as something to attract, have sex with, and then move on. This was the mentality I had adopted from my peers and, I suppose, on a level, from adverse experiences in my childhood. I never had competent carers to talk to me about relationships and teach me about morals and ethics, so I just saw this way of seeing girls as normal and meeting my own desire for gratification. What Laura didn't know at the time was that she was about to change my mindset completely.

It was evident to see that Laura's nature and persona were placid, nurturing, caring, and calm. Something felt very different with Laura; she was very understanding towards me and listened well. It felt like I could learn to love her, even though my blueprint of intimate relationships was obscure and somewhat clouded. I believed I could learn to be with someone who would love me for all my faults, scars, and imperfections, despite my bravado and cheeky smile.

By the time I came to leave DHL, Laura and I had been dating for nearly a month, and at the time, I had my own flat in Birmingham, which I shared with someone I used to live in care with. Laura introduced me to her parents, and then, within a matter of weeks, I was staying over at her house on weekends. It transpired that my flatmate needed a permanent residence, and I was spending more and more time over at Laura's parents' house, so we decided to put the rented flat in his name, and I moved in with Laura and her family permanently.

Her family were super supportive towards me, and I could see that Laura had two loving and caring parents with three siblings—two sisters and a brother. It was everything I had hoped for in a family: the togetherness, the love, the warmth. Laura and I shared her bedroom, and we spent long periods of time watching movies and series with each other. Our favourite series were *The Walking Dead* and *Spartacus*. We would get super excited for the next week to come so we could find out what the cliffhanger had in store. I was doing well in my new role as a residential support worker, and life just seemed to be settled, coming from a life that had been very unsettled and somewhat chaotic and turbulent.

And then one day, those famous two words came out of Laura's mouth:

"I'm pregnant."

All I remember in the moment was this selfish, self-protective side of me coming out and saying, "Are you keeping it?"

At 23 years of age, I didn't want to become a dad. I didn't want to become a parent. I felt like my entire life would be over if she did decide to keep the baby. Laura had been using the contraceptive pill; however, she had been sick for a few days after, so the pill had not been effective, hence her pregnancy. I was so fearful of becoming a dad. I felt this decision should be both of ours to make.

She told me that she would be having the baby, and that I had to decide whether I wanted to be with her or not. So, I remember jumping into my Vauxhall Corsa car and driving straight over to Dave's house.

He opened the door, and he could see I was flustered. He asked me if everything was okay. I said, "No, Laura's pregnant." He smiled and said, "Surely this is good news!" I said, "I'm not sure, Dave; I'm not sure I'm ready to be a dad." Then he looked me in my eyes and said, "Steven, you may not be ready to be a dad, but your child is ready for you to be a dad."

I had no response to that statement. We sat and talked, as Dave and I do, and once again, he helped to bring me around to the idea of becoming a dad, and to become the dad that I never had. "Yes, it will be difficult," he said, "but you have the opportunity to raise your own child, given all of your experiences in life as a child in care, and to be the parent to him you always wished you'd had."

Over the coming months, I noticed Laura's belly getting bigger and bigger, and I would rest my head on her belly to hear the baby moving around. I would talk to her belly, and I would rub bio-oil into her skin. I found myself late-night shopping in Asda to buy baby items such as nappies, toys, and baby milk.

I was becoming excited about the prospect of becoming a dad.

We were able to find out the sex of the baby. Even though I wanted to be surprised at the birth, Laura wanted to know, so I thought, *If you're going to know, I may as well find out too.* So, we found out the baby was going to be a boy.

All that was left to do, as Laura went through her final stages of pregnancy, was to think of a name for the baby. Maybe it was Dave's inspiration—I'm not sure—but we found ourselves in bed looking through the Bible at names. We initially liked the name "Micah," but then changed our minds when we flicked the page over to the book of "Malachi," meaning "The messenger of God."

It was a winner, and something we were both happy with. As Laura's belly grew, so did the name on us both. Malachi was perfect.

Malachi was born onto the earth in April 2009. Laura's labour lasted for approximately 15 hours, and there were some complications during the birth. We had our bags packed and were scheduled for a water birth; however, this did not go to plan. Malachi had become entangled in the umbilical cord as Laura was preparing to give birth, which meant she was taken down for an emergency caesarean to have Malachi delivered.

It was a highly stressful and worrying time because all I remember seeing was a lot of blood on the bed Laura was lying on, with multiple nurses and doctors rushing around to move the bed to another ward. I had a horrible feeling that one of them might die. It was such a frantic experience, and I just remember feeling helpless!

And then, the moment came. The nurse wheeled a small incubator into the room where Laura's mum and I were waiting and said, "He's a healthy, 8lb boy, and Laura is recovering well in intensive care."

At this point, Malachi was 10 minutes old.

I wanted to give Laura's mum the first opportunity to hold Malachi because I felt it should have been Laura's right, but she was unable to.

And then came the moment I had been anticipating I was about to hold my child for the first time. Laura's mum handed Malachi over to me, and I remember feeling so nervous and excited at the same time. I still can't explain the feeling I had, but it was like I had been climbing a mountain my whole life—through care, through the pain and the rejections—and I reached the top of this mountain to find a baby boy waiting for me to be his dad.

When Laura had finally come around from theatre, she was presented with Malachi. She was so tired and drained but still found the energy to hold her newborn son, smiling from ear to ear.

Laura and Malachi were kept in hospital under observation for an additional few days before they were allowed to leave.

As soon as we pulled out of the hospital, my car began to make a noise, and there was a funny smell that reminded me of when my clutch went on a previous car. Then, of course, the gears stopped working, so I had to pull the car over to the side of the road. I immediately had my first fearful moment as a parent and just wanted to protect my newborn baby and his mother. I perceived the threat of breaking down, so we phoned Laura's dad, and he immediately came out in his car to collect Laura and Malachi while I waited with the car to be picked up.

All in all, Malachi was safe, Laura was safe, and that's all that mattered to me.

It's true—nothing can prepare you for being a parent. No books, no courses, no previous parents' advice. It's a whole new journey you must embark on together—or, in some people's cases, alone.

It kind of felt like Laura and I were fumbling around in the dark looking after this newborn baby, but with the help of Laura's parents, Dave, and my ex-foster carers Eunice and Neville, we were in very good hands. I remember us giving

Malachi his very first bath, and we were constantly checking the temperature of the water. It was the cutest thing ever—his tiny little body, arms, and legs. He was screaming, and then he began to settle as we submerged him into the water.

(Scan QR code to see video)

Like most babies, I guess, Malachi struggled to go to sleep, so we tried different ways to help him. The car was always a winner in that respect—he would nod off to sleep almost straight away once the movement of the car gained momentum. Another way that worked well was bouncing him on the gym ball with a soft muslin cloth wrapped around him. I would sing him nursery rhymes; his favourite seemed to be *This Old Man*.

I suppose what I'm saying here is, I never had a clue what I was doing—like most new parents. Laura had grown up with her parents, so she had some inclination of what to do from that perspective, whereas my parental blueprint was non-existent. I was playing the role of what I thought a dad should do.

So now Laura and I were in the full swing of parent life. We were talking about the idea of having more children, and we thought, *If we're going to have just two children, why not have them close together in age?* This was the line of thinking behind Cory.

And so, within a few months, Laura became pregnant with Cory. Like with Malachi, she had to have a planned caesarean due to the previous complications. The whole pregnancy went well, as did Cory's birth in May 2010.

We first noticed his red hair and wondered where he might have got that from. Then I remembered—my mother's hair is naturally red. Laura has blonde hair, and I have brown hair.

Quick fact:

The surname Russell comes from Scotland but is derived from Normandy in France. Way back in the 1300s, it was pronounced "Rousel."

Rousel in French means "little redhead."

So, Cory is an original Russell—or should I say Rousel.

As I mentioned earlier, Cory and I have a particular affinity for each other. He is so creative and clever, which is something I noticed when he was a toddler. He would always want to make things, particularly out of boxes. He loved to create and see how things worked. If ever there was a large box—say, from a new TV—he would immediately become excited about it and play with it for days.

I spent most of Cory's childhood making him laugh, giggling, and having fun. It's also the reason why my prediction was correct about how each child would react to the news that their mum and I were breaking up.

Eventually, Cory came back downstairs and said he wanted to go out to see his friend Logan. I understood he needed some space and time to reflect on the devastating news he had just received. And so, I hugged him as we sat on the stairs and whispered into his ear, "I'm so sorry."

I could no longer hold my tears in—they had already filled to the top of my cup—so I released them with him. I think he may have appreciated my true emotion being released because it matched his own sadness.

And then there's Alyssa, my beautiful, intelligent daughter.

Alyssa was born in August 2012.

I remember being super excited when I found out I was going to have a baby girl. I remember Alyssa being born, again by planned caesarean like Cory. I just found Alyssa to be adorable and wanted to hold and play with her all the time.

I found it so cute how the boys would interact with her, sitting and holding her in the hospital. Malachi would sing her a song, which was so beautiful to see—ever the protector and the leader. *(Scan QR code to view video)*

As Alyssa grew, I noticed more and more how my affinity and protection for her grew. I was always unsure of where this affinity came from. I just knew it was very different to the boys and still is to this day. Alyssa holds a very special part of my heart, and yes, part of it may be because she is my only girl, or it may just be because she is the youngest of my children, and I have struggled to let go of my "baby," so to speak.

Those would be practical reasons, I suppose. However, I feel so much more than that—almost on a spiritual level—so I literally can't find the words to explain the feeling.

Due to Alyssa's birthday, she is one of the youngest in her class at school. Had she been born three days later, she would have been in the year below. Alyssa has always shown strong levels of emotional intelligence, and I don't think it's done her any harm to be the youngest in her class. She has had to learn and adapt with children who are older than her, and yet her feisty, sassy nature has held her in good stead.

I love Alyssa's nature. She is sharp and witty, yet emotionally aware of the people around her.

So, I now understand why her initial reaction to the news of me leaving the family home was masked with a smile—she didn't know any other way to express her emotions at the time. I suppose, out of the three children, Alyssa has responded in the most assured way. She even came over to my new place of residence to help me unpack and set the room out, which she seemed to really enjoy despite the anguish and pain that was attached.

So, the reason this chapter is called *Torn* is because that's exactly how I felt going through this process—emotionally, mentally, physically and spiritually torn.

Aside from the most significant tear, which is my children, there was also the tear between Laura and me parting ways after 16 years together; the tear from the house we had built over 13 years; the financial tear, having to pay rent after so many years of investing into our own mortgage; and the spiritual tear, which is equally as significant as the tear from my children.

Little Steven—his lifelong mission as a child was to find his own family, and I believe this was achieved the day Malachi was born onto the earth. It was a groundbreaking day for me on so many levels. Up until this point in time, I had already lived with 10 foster families and two care homes, so rejection was already built into my blueprint.

It felt like I could rip that blueprint up now that I had made my own family. Then Cory came along. Then we started our mortgage together in our family home. And then Alyssa came along to add the final piece.

So, as we end on this chapter, I am sure you are wondering at this stage: *Why? Steven, why would you leave your family when you had spent your lifetime searching for what you are now leaving? Why walk away from your children, your home, and such a beautiful human in Laura, who has done nothing but support you? Why leave behind your home and everything you have spent so long working for and building? Surely, Steven, you won the game of life. You defeated all those odds to achieve the greatest prize of all—your own family. So why go?*

It would be a fair question to ask, given the journey I have been on.

The truth is, I was selfish, I took advantage of my family, and I allowed my dark side to take control of my responses far too many times. And as much as Laura loved me, she always knew my love for her could not be reciprocated in the same way. She accepted that and made up for the percentage of love I struggled to give. This is why she is incredible and such a beautiful human being.

The only way I can describe my rationale for leaving is that I had become unavailable and emotionally distant and so I buried myself in work, and then when *Elements* came along, I poured so much energy into it that there wasn't much left over for them. I allowed the selfish subtract of my dark side to ensure I was achieving my goals and dreams. Naturally, I would then feel guilty. I would try to be there with them, but there has always been this need for me to be isolated from everyone—a need to be solitary and alone.

This is my blueprint. This is my natural state of being: to be with myself, not necessarily by myself.

So, I found myself turning down family events or Christmas gatherings when everyone would go around to Laura's parents' house for dinner. I would refuse to go because I preferred to be by myself. It was self-fulfilling—this was me meeting my own needs, I suppose.

Six years prior to Laura and me breaking up, we had gone through our first separation, and I moved out into rented accommodation. I remember feeling a sense of liberation, running free as a bachelor. Then, in the space of months, I became extremely uncomfortable with the loneliness, and I wanted to be around my family again. So, Laura and I decided I should move back in.

But I realise now that the gap that had developed between Laura and me was still there—and growing. I went back for my children to have their dad back in the house. And so, six years passed, and I came to this realisation that my deeper inner feelings were saying:

Steven, you need to leave. This isn't working. How much longer are you prepared to pretend everything's okay, and everything will continue to be okay? You are the children's dad. They need you in their lives, but not like this. You are no longer present, and you have become distant and unavailable for your children. So, leave, and clear your head and be the dad your children deserve while you co-parent with Laura and ensure she feels supported.

My consensus is this: Love is not enough. In an ideal world, it would be, but it's not. For a relationship to truly work, we need emotional maturity, self-awareness, conflict resolution skills, compassionate empathy, attentive listening, and effective communication. Love alone simply isn't sufficient.

Upon reflection, I now realise that I lacked so many of these skills when I entered the relationship at 22. There was no real pace to it, no time taken to properly get to know one another. Everything moved far too quickly. As a result, while we endured in the relationship, it wasn't built on a strong enough foundation.

Children need their parents—absolutely, 100%. But they don't need their parents to pretend everything is fine when it's clearly not. If the environment becomes toxic, then it's our responsibility to change it. However, in this case, it wasn't the environment that was the issue—it was me being in it. It may feel daunting, frightening, and, in some ways, like failure. I certainly felt like a failure to my children as a father. Yet, I knew that the long-term result would bring greater peace and harmony for everyone.

Drip by drip, day by day—this has never been more relevant to me than in my relationship with my children. Even though I no longer live with them in the family home, I will *always* be available. I will *always* be in their corner. Just because I've left doesn't mean the care has left. I will stand by their side until my very last breath.

Drip By Drip Day By Day

Steven Russell

Thirteen

Melting The Ice

I believe life is a dream, a delicate balance between positive and negative, light and dark, good and evil - mirroring life itself. With every sunrise comes the sunset. After every night, the dawn breaks. Seasons change in their inevitable cycle, from summer to winter, and from winter to spring. Our lives mirror these simple truths, a dance of ups and downs, guided by luck, God, or the universe. No amount of money can shield us from these universal truths.

Let me delve deeper into my thoughts with quotes from remarkable individuals who have fuelled my inner fire and inspired me to soar higher, pushing me to become the best version of myself, unapologetically.

> "You don't have to be great to start, but you do have to start to be great."
> – Les Brown

Les Brown, an American motivational speaker, entered my life in 2017 via cassette tapes. A time when I was feeling lost and dissatisfied with my life path. Despite sensing greatness within me, I struggled to unleash it. Contemplating the idea of starting my own children's support service, I was clueless about its name, purpose, and how to begin.

One evening, while returning from work in the car, I stumbled upon a Les Brown YouTube video. His words struck a chord as he emphasised that greatness stems from taking that initial step, not from waiting for perfection. This message resonated deeply, igniting a spark within me.

Channelling the determination of my youth when I crafted plans to transform my life. I grabbed a plain notebook from *Hobbycraft*, labelling it "Ideas Book." I filled its pages with insights, quotes, and visions inspired by Les Brown and my own thoughts. Drip by drip, over five years, these scribbles evolved into the blueprint for what would later materialise as the Elements Support Community Interest Company.

If you're feeling lost, uncertain, or unsure right now, remember, there's so much more inside you waiting to shine through. Try what worked for me - a journal, blank pages, and a pen. The blank page mirrored my mind initially, but as I went about my daily routine, interacting with the children I was supporting in residential homes, networking with professionals, and engaging on LinkedIn, ideas poured in like a river of knowledge. Putting pen to paper led me to the first project I wanted to launch in schools. Keep exploring your potential!

With every new endeavour come sceptics, naysayers, and closed doors. Rejections and uncertainties may make you second-guess your mission and direction. But remember, when you cast your hook into the sea of opportunities, the universe whispers, "How badly do you want this?" Many falter at this point, succumbing to fear and self-doubt. Don't be one of them. Persist like I did, knocking on doors despite the "No thank you's." Trust the voice inside you that says, "It will happen, just keep going." The universe is testing your resolve; show it how much you truly desire success. Stay the course, and your breakthrough will surely come.

If you knock on 100 doors and none open, keep the mindset: "I'll knock on 100 more." Persist until someone responds. Even if they decline, greet them warmly. Show humility, gratitude, and appreciation. The universe hears you. One day, a door may open, offering a lead. Remember, as Les Brown said, "You don't have to be great to start, but you have to start to be great." Five years later, I feel greater than I have ever felt!

The journey to success is not always a smooth one. It is filled with challenges, setbacks, and obstacles that can make you question your abilities and goals. But it is important to remember that every successful person has faced their fair share of struggles before achieving their dreams.

As an entrepreneur or someone pursuing their passion, it is crucial to have a strong support system in place. Surround yourself with people who believe in you and your potential, who will lift you up when you feel down and inspire you to keep going. This could be friends, family, mentors, or other like-minded individuals.

It is important to continuously learn and grow. Success is not a destination but a journey, and it requires constant improvement and adaptation. Be open to new ideas, experiences, and perspectives. Invest in your personal and professional development to become the best version of yourself.

Don't be afraid to take risks and step out of your comfort zone. Success often requires taking bold and unconventional actions. Embrace failure as a learning opportunity and use it to propel yourself forward.

Remember that success is not just about achieving material wealth or status. It is also about finding fulfilment and purpose in what you do. Reflect on your values, passions, and goals. Align your actions with your true desires, and success will follow.

And most importantly, always stay true to yourself. Don't let societal expectations or external pressures dictate your path to success. Stay authentic and genuine, and the universe will reward you with true success.

In conclusion, no one's journey to success is the same. It is a unique and personal experience, filled with ups and downs. But by having a strong support system, continuously learning, and growing, taking risks, staying aligned with your values, and staying authentic, you can overcome any obstacles and achieve your dreams. So, keep pushing forward and never give up on your dream.

"You can't stop the waves, but you can learn to surf," – Jon Kabat Zinn

Jon Founded the globally recognised Mindfulness-Based Stress Reduction (MBSR) practice, now embraced worldwide.

It was a young person who initially shared this quote with me during my time supporting them in high school. The project aimed to encourage introspection on a quote that deeply connects with their personal journey. This young person crafted a canvas portraying a sunset, waves, and themselves on the shore. When asked about the quote's significance, they expressed that it's our ability to navigate life's challenges that truly shape us.

I couldn't shake the feeling of how incredibly true this quote is and how deeply it resonates with me on personal, professional, and spiritual levels. Reflecting on my childhood within the care system, I realised that many of the hurdles I faced weren't my doing.

Yet, I was expected to navigate through them. Those barriers, like relentless waves, tossed me between foster homes. Each new placement bringing unfamiliar faces, painful goodbyes, and the constant sting of rejection. As I stand here today, I see those painful experiences as essential in shaping who I've become - someone who turned their pain into purpose. I've learned to ride those waves, and I know many of you can relate. Life throws challenge our way, making us stumble off our surfboards, but we gather the courage to hop back on. It's a dance between facing challenges and finding the strength to rise again. Every high wave we surf is a victory, preparing us for the next one that looms on the horizon. Life's waves keep coming, but mastering the art of surfing them not only equips us to tackle challenges head-on but also teaches our children the same resilience and fortitude.

The process of learning to ride life's waves isn't an easy one. It requires a lot of strength, determination, and resilience. But the rewards are immeasurable. Not only do we become stronger individuals ourselves, but we also set an example for those around us - our children, our families, our friends.

As we navigate through the challenge and uncertainty that comes our way, we also develop important life skills, such as problem-solving, adaptability, and perseverance. These skills are crucial not only in overcoming obstacles but also in achieving success and reaching our goals.

Learning to ride the waves of life also teaches us the importance of self-care and self-compassion. We learn that it's okay to fall off our surfboards sometimes, to take a break and recharge before getting back up again. We learn to listen to our bodies and minds, taking care of ourselves so that we can continue to face life's challenges with strength and resilience.

So, as we continue our journey through life, let's remember that every wave we ride is an opportunity for growth and development. Let's embrace the uncertainty, pain, and struggles, knowing that they will only strengthen us in the end. And let's pass on this valuable lesson to those around us, creating a ripple effect of resilience and fortitude for generations to come.

Life is like an endless ocean, with its ups and downs. But as long as we have the courage and determination to ride its waves, we can conquer anything that comes our way. So, let's keep surfing, learning, and growing, always striving to become the best versions of ourselves. And in doing so, we'll not only navigate through life successfully, but also inspire our children to do the same.

> **"It's not the time you put in that matters, it's what you put into the time that counts."**
> **– Jim Rohn**

Jim Rohn was an American entrepreneur, author, and motivational speaker.

I first came across this quote by Jim Rohn in a YouTube video. He emphasised the importance of quality in our work, relationships, parenthood, and business endeavours. The quote highlights the significance of choosing quality over quantity, urging us to embody it in both our thoughts and actions. Rohn's message resonated deeply with me during a pivotal moment in my life. This quote transcends various roles, stressing that true value is not just in the time spent, but in the quality of our efforts within that period.

We often link time with progress, assuming that more time leads to better results. However, my experiences working with children and young people have shown me that even brief interactions can have a meaningful impact. The magic is in the energy, passion, and positivity we put into shared moments, big or small—from playtime to school walks to dinner conversations. By prioritising quality in our interactions and endeavours, we lay the groundwork for more positive outcomes - benefiting not only ourselves but also our communities, friends, and families.

In today's fast-paced world, it's tempting to do more in less time. We frequently prioritise quantity over quality, chasing instant gratification and swift outcomes. Yet, this approach can lead to burnout and a lack of satisfaction in our work and relationships. Rohn's quote serves as a gentle nudge to slow down and focus on delivering our best in all that we do. By doing so, we can nurture a sense of purpose and fulfilment, rather than merely checking tasks off our to-do list.

Prioritising quality enables us to make a lasting impact and form meaningful connections with those around us. In today's digital era, relationships can feel superficial. So, it's crucial to remember the value of quality time and genuine human connection. By investing in the quality of our interactions, we can cultivate deeper understanding, trust, and empathy. This not only benefits us personally but also ripples out to society as a whole. Genuine connections enable us to learn, evolve, and effect positive change in the world.

"You can't pour from an empty cup, and you can't fill a cup that is already full." – unknown

This is a two-part quote that weaves together two contrasting yet profound ideas. Imagine this: the notion of not being able to pour from an empty cup. It's about lacking the energy to give to others, work, family, friends, relationships, or anything external. How can we authentically offer what we lack for ourselves? On the flip side, picture a cup already full. If we're swamped, overwhelmed, with deadlines piling up, it's equally tough to make space for ourselves. Balancing our well-being becomes crucial amidst life's chaos.

From a turbulent childhood in the care system, I learned to rely on myself, crafting a shield of self-reliance. Enduring multiple moves, broken attachments, and shattered trust, I found solace in my own company. Despite the solitude, this journey taught me resilience and self-preservation. Prioritising self-care isn't selfish; it's a foundation for giving back authentically. By nurturing our well-being first, we empower ourselves to positively impact others.

Dear reader, when was the last time you did something solely for yourself? Reflect on what ignites your joy, fulfils your soul, and fuels your purpose. Take a moment to replenish your cup, find pride in your worth, and embrace the truth that you are significant. Remember, by filling your own cup, you'll overflow with the energy needed to inspire, influence, and impact the lives around you.

The idea of caring for ourselves before others may seem counterintuitive. But it's crucial for maintaining our mental and emotional well-being. By prioritising self-care, we can show up fully for the people and responsibilities in our lives.

Self-care varies for everyone, and it's essential to find what works best for you. For some, it may mean dedicating time each day to meditation or mindfulness. For others, it could involve indulging in a hobby or passion project. Whatever form of self-care resonates with you, prioritise it in your life.

Self-care isn't just about pampering ourselves; it also includes setting boundaries and prioritising our needs. Recognise when to step back and recharge, whether it's from work, relationships, or stressors. By setting boundaries and learning to say no to things that don't serve us, we actively practice self-care.

Ultimately, self-care is about finding balance in our lives and caring for ourselves physically, emotionally, and spiritually. It's an ongoing practice that requires mindfulness and self-awareness. When we make self-care a priority, we're better able to support ourselves and those in our lives. So, when you feel guilty for putting yourself first, remember that self-care isn't selfish; it's necessary.

"If you want to take the island, burn the boats" – Tony Robbins

Tony Robbins is a world-renowned motivational business guru from America.

Once, I came across the idea that there exists a fine line between knowledge and action. It dawned on me that each of us is aware of what we should do to lead a more fulfilling life. We understand that sugar is detrimental to our bodies, yet we give in to that tempting donut. We know that alcohol, cigarettes, and vaping are harmful, but we still indulge. We recognise that disrespect and belittling others only breed toxicity in relationships, yet some of us resist changing our behaviour. It seems that, for the majority; the challenge lies not in knowing what to do, but in taking action, assuming control, and owning up to our responsibilities.

My exposure to motivational speakers like Les Brown, Jim Rohn, Simon Sinek, and Mel Robbins has been enlightening. However, Tony Robbins was one of the first speakers I encountered in the realm of self-improvement. In one of his seminars on YouTube, he used a striking phrase that initially puzzled me: "If you want to take the island, you have to burn the boats." As I delved into its meaning, I interpreted it as a metaphor for the distinction between knowing and doing.

As a young man finishing school without GCSEs, plagued by a negative attitude, indulging in cannabis and alcohol each weekend, I found myself behaving foolishly. Despite my delinquent actions, a small inner voice reminded me of right and wrong. Highlighting the disparity between my behaviours and the person I aspired to be. Walking through life with a heavy chip on my shoulder, a product of the care system, I once believed the world owed me something. It took years to realise that the world had already provided me with all I needed; I simply failed to recognise it. Reflecting on a near-death experience at 20, following a stabbing incident. I embraced Les Brown's wisdom: *to succeed, one must possess a deep hunger for success, determination to overcome adversity, pain, and rejection.* At that pivotal moment, I understood the necessity of being hungry, ready to burn the boats and commit fully to my transformation.

My interpretation of Tony Robbins' phrase "if you want to take the island, you have to burn the boats" is that it signifies a total commitment. The island symbolises success, achievement, and reaching the pinnacle. On the other hand, the boat represents regression, half-hearted commitments, and a temptation to return to the past. By burning the boats, you make a firm decision to never go back to the life you left behind, regardless of what challenges come your way. I chose to leave behind adversity, pain, rejection, substance abuse, unhealthy habits, toxic people, purposeless environments, excuses, and any negativity that weighed me down.

Burning the boats symbolises a deep commitment to progress and growth, ushering in a new way of living. It's not about mere necessity or convenience; it's about a resolute sense of purpose. I firmly believe that when you shift from something you "should" do to something you "must" do, you propel yourself towards greatness, tapping into the greatness that already resides within you.

At age 20, I burnt the boats. I did not know what awaited me on that unknown island, its size, its inhabitants, its weather. Uncertainty loomed, yet turning back was too easy, too safe. It reminds me of a powerful quote by Les Brown: "In life, if you do what's easy, your life will be hard. But if you do what's hard, your life will be easy." I knew this was a tough choice. Let's be clear, making significant life changes isn't a walk in the park. If it were easy to give up sugar, smoking, vaping, alcohol, or to rein in your emotions, everyone would do it. But the truth is, the path to transformation is challenging precisely because it's not meant for everyone.

It all boils down to mindset - the mindset we nurture within ourselves to tackle tough decisions. The person I am today is a product of the choices I made yesterday. Born from a commitment to burn the boats and eliminate the option to revert to a purposeless life. This is where self-belief takes root, self-esteem flourishes, and we empower ourselves to a place of strength. Regardless of any negative feedback or discouraging words aimed at blocking our progress. We listen, show respect, yet acknowledge that our true growth lies within us, not in others. A memorable moment from the movie "The Pursuit of Happyness'" echoes in my mind. It's the scene on the basketball court where Will Smith's character imparts wisdom to his son.

"Don't ever let somebody tell you, you can't do something. If you got a dream you've got to protect it. When people can't do something themselves, they want to tell you, you can't do it, so if you want something, go get it."

These words hold true in life as well. Often, we let others' opinions and doubts dictate our actions, leading us to give up on our dreams or goals. But the truth is, no one can stop us from achieving what we truly desire except for ourselves. This is where resilience comes into play. Resilience is not about being invincible or never feeling pain - it's about being able to bounce back from setbacks and continue moving forward. It's the ability to pick ourselves up after we fall, learn from our mistakes, and keep going. Resilience is a crucial characteristic that helps us stay committed to our goals despite obstacles or challenges along the way. Without resilience, we may be more likely to give up when things get tough.

Fourteen

Living In My Shadow

Everyone has a dark side right! I like to call it my shadow, the dark side of me that follows me around everywhere I go.

I mean, we all have a capacity for anger, sin, envy, hate and being ego-centric alongside narcissistic self-absorbed traits.

We live in a world of masks, smoke screens, and happy filters, where we want people to like us, respect us and hold us in high regard. It takes a great deal of courage and vulnerability to admit one's flaws, imperfections, and weaknesses as it goes way outside of the social norms. After all, Society expects us to be strong, clean, presentable, and to maintain appearances or even to keep up with the Joneses.

Isn't it sad that the one life we have is to be a fabricated, fake, filtered version of ourselves, instead of our authentic, organismic, imperfect human selves?

Well, I decided with this book that I would embrace my vulnerability to allow you to see that it's okay to embrace your dark side, your shadow, and your imperfections. After all, behind the mask, behind the filter, there you are!

So how would I describe my shadow, my dark side? What an interesting question to ask someone, *"How would you describe your dark side?"* It feels like I must work hard to keep my shadow in check, not run away from it, but work with it daily. I suppose a better question to ask is this. What would it look like if my dark side was in full control all day, every day?

Well, I would see everyone as an immediate threat. I would go to war with anyone who disagreed with me, and I would attempt to control every situation around me. I would use people to get ahead in life, then cast them away once I no longer had any use for them. I wouldn't have any friends or people close to me. I'd tell my children daily how lucky they are to have me but would only spend time with them when I chose. I would cheat on my partner and use women for gratification to suit my own sexual needs. I would be selfish with my time, and it would be known that I am the most important person in the room. I am the centre of attention and no one's feelings matter except my own. I would be consumed and absorbed within my shadow, and I would spew hot venom at anyone who tried to tell me I was wrong. It would be total self-absorption with zero empathy, zero compassion and zero respect for other people. I would allow my narcissistic traits to overspill into the world, causing further damage to my relationships. It wouldn't be long before I am alone and lonely simultaneously in a dark room cramped within the walls of my own mind until the day I die. It would be a living hell situation! Which I suppose is the point, isn't it?

We all have this dark capability inside us, and deep down, we all know it's true. We just choose not to talk about our shadows, our dark side. Instead, we profess and pretend everything is okay. We're all good, honest citizens doing the right thing in our angelic way. None of us has darkness within us. But this is not reality, is it?

What does my dark side look like?

I think most people would struggle with that question, not because they don't know the answers, because they do. Everyone knows there's something about them that's not good, not great, nor amazing. The issue with the question would be the comprehension of the question, i.e. *How do I answer this question without my entire sense of self falling apart?*

Did you know that the word *Narcissism* came from the roman poet Ovid's Metamorphoses? He wrote a poem in the year 8 AD which told the mythical story of a handsome young man called Narcissus. Narcissus fell in love with his own reflection and lived out the rest of his life completely self-absorbed and consumed by himself. The term narcissism comes from the Greek word "Narkissos" which means "Self-Love."

So, whilst the word Narcissism in popular culture today has a very negative tone to it, there is also a healthy side to narcissism as it refers to loving oneself, which, of course, is a good thing. However, Narcissism, like most human conditions, is on a continuum, meaning every one of us is on the spectrum to some varying degree, however NPD (Narcissistic Personality Disorder) is something entirely separate and far more harmful to relationships.

I know I have narcissistic tendencies; my shadow reminds me all the time that I need to be self-absorbed. My feelings matter the most. Look after number one. So, I must combat this with intention. I have to go against this dark side and become more people centric instead of steven centric. So, I do small things like give people a listening ear, or I bring treats back for my children on a Friday night, or I will take the kids out for a meal or to play bowling. I am conscious of the balance between light and dark and I feel this is the only way I can keep the dark side in check.

When I cast my mind over the years and think about all of the negative phrases I have been called, the common theme has always been.

"You're selfish. You only think about yourself."

And it really pains me to know there is a huge element of truth to this. It's no secret that our experiences in early childhood literally impact our adult selves, especially where attachment theory is concerned, and of course Maslow's hierarchy of needs. My relationships with other people as a child were extremely disorganised, and, of course, this was going to have a detrimental effect on my relationships later on in life, as I became an adult through adolescence. All I ever knew as a child was to look out for me. 10 foster homes, two care homes and five schools will certainly do that for a child. It was always just me with and by myself. I even created an imaginary friend called John because I felt so alone. I could talk to my imagination, play, and entertain myself, because I had no choice but to be with myself. I never had siblings, and any friends I made at school were quickly taken away when I had to move homes. So, I learned, people were only there temporarily. They would never be permanent fixtures in my life, like a typical family that goes through thick and thin together. And so, I became my own best friend. I looked out for me, and I ensured my emotional needs were met; I soothed myself at night, crying on my blue bear, and god knows how many different pillows.

So today, as an adult, I must work extra hard to tell little Steven we are okay, and that there is no threat here. Isn't it funny how other people, systems, media etc. can evoke and trigger our emotions, simply based on something we may have experienced as children, and so we act childishly, or we perform immaturely. We see and feel this through emails and text messages, which are sugar-coated with emojis so the receiver can see where our emotions are at.

My shadow is impatient and often shows a lack of tolerance, empathy, and understanding for others' disposition. Some may even wonder how I can do what I do in supporting children in care, or support families on the brink of destruction and, to me, it's really quite simple. I can feel their pain through my own experiences.

I can embrace compassionate empathy through my own experiences of loneliness, rejection, and suffering. Not only do I genuinely love what I do, I enjoy the challenge adversity offers. So, the way it works is, adversity is a dark cloud that looms over many children in care and I have a dark side that I can control, so alongside my light side, it actually becomes quite a potent force for good. And we see this occur with fictional characters such as Harry Potter. Harry has a dark side within him which is connected through Voldemort. However, Harry finds new ways to defeat Voldemort by using his own powers against him. We see this with batman; we see this with Dr Jekyll and Hyde, and we see this with the incredible Hulk. All these characters have dark sides they must contend with and the potential to cause harm. They are forever with them and might consume them. However, they have found ways to work alongside the dark side for the greater good. I certainly do not see myself as a caped superhero when it comes to championing children in care, but what I see myself as is imperfect. I know I will make mistakes; I will get things wrong but my willingness to fail is immeasurable.

So, despite my dark side, despite my shadow, I now know who I am and what I am capable of. I have already proven it with the people I have supported since 2006; the children, the families, the teachers, and the communities who I have had the privilege of being with. My shadow is very much like fire (And for all those astrologists out there, you may have noticed I am indeed a Leo star sign, which is a fire sign).

A fire left unchecked will cause mass destruction, cause immense pain, and will destroy and rage through the night. However, a fire that is in check will provide warmth, light and comfort for all those who need it. It will melt the ice away, drip By Drip Day By Day. So, my mission is pretty simple, do something every day to ensure the balance is tipped towards the latter, because the alternative is not good news for anyone, including myself.

How did my shadow manifest as a child? Vengeance was a dangerous thought process for me, especially if I felt threatened.

I remember when I was six years old at school. A few of the children in my class would laugh at me because they knew Pat (My foster mum) wasn't my real mum. So, I decided I would seek vengeance against Luke, who was the ringleader laughing at me. So, I waited until break time and planned to cause him pain. I went into the toilets, took some sheets of the blue paper towels, soaked them in water, then rubbed soap into the wet paper towel with a grin on my face. I walked up to Luke in the playground with my hands behind my back, then slapped the flattened wet soapy paper towel into his eye. He then ran off screaming, "I can't see!" Much to my delight.

I suppose what this taught me was not to tell other children in school that I lived in care. I was genuinely scared about people finding out because I feared the other children would bully me for it. I have always had this feeling that I need to protect myself from people because no one was going to protect me; I learnt to become comfortable in my own skin and began to talk to myself as if I were my own best friend. I knew my creativity could manifest into something beautiful or something callous and evil depending on my state of mood.

The more I moved homes, the more evil thoughts I would have. It felt as though no one cared about me, so I decided not to care about anyone else. I became selfish and bitter and only thought about my own wellbeing to ensure my needs were met. When my mum used to visit me, I would often give her a hard time because I had no connection to her whatsoever. I would often scream in public, "Help! She's trying to kidnap me!" I mean, how embarrassing must this have been for my mum? When I consider little Steven's behaviour, I see it as a reflection of his feelings. Yet he faced criticism and ridicule from adults, who then accused him of disrespecting my mother. As a child, my vengeance would be subtle. I would remember you hurt me and then get you back when you least expect it. So, from spitting in your well mixed hot chocolate to drawing pins underneath your bedsheets, I had my creative ways of getting you back.

My cry was very much one of, "How dare you treat me like this? Let's see how you like it."

When I moved to my final care home at 12, I was about to learn a whole new level of payback, because I was now living with seven other young boys who were of a similar mind to me, so of course we would get up to lots of creative ways to pay each other back, but together we were formidable and quickly gained reputations around the Castle Vale estate.

Setting fires was a regular activity for us. We liked the idea of blowing things up. So, we would ask willing adults to buy us fireworks from the shops (can you believe these adults would buy children, cigarettes, alcohol, and fireworks?)

Then I thought it was super cool, but now I think, *how could you do that to a child?* So, we would go onto double-decker buses, light fireworks then throw them out of the window by passers-by. Our favourite thing to do was to light fireworks, then post them into people's houses. Yeah, not your average knock door run. We would put broken pieces of slabs onto railway tracks and balance metal rods on cups in the road. Once we made a car swerve into the curb, almost causing them to crash.

One of the local girls on the estate invited us all over to her mom's flat one night when she had a free yard (An available place to stay). Someone dared me to throw this broken TV off the side of the balcony, bearing in mind we were on the top floor of this high-rise flat. Anyway, when someone dared you to do something back in the noughties, you just had to do it, no matter what. So here I am, balancing this large TV on the balcony of this high-rise flat. All I could see at the bottom was how small the cars were and it was nighttime. PUSH! Off the TV goes, hurtling towards the ground at God knows what speed. I felt a powerful adrenaline rush. SMASH! Onto the ground. We're all giggling and laughing. Then we hear a voice of an angry man from the ground, "You wait until I find your fucking door number!"

We are all now fearful of what this fully grown adult male will do to us if he finds out what flat we are in. Moments later, BANG! BANG! BANG! on the door. We were all officially shitting ourselves at this point. "You can either open the door, or I'm kicking it off!" said the voice of the angry male outside of the flat door.

The girl who lived at the flat said she had to open the door because she didn't want her mum coming back to a broken door, so she tried speaking to him through the chained door, but he aggressively demanded to be let in. He entered the flat and was clearly quite upset. "Who the fuck just threw the TV off the balcony?"

Every one of us was frozen at this point! What I failed to mention was, he had a small child with him and he said, "If me and my daughter had walked out of the building seconds before, you would have killed us! You're fuckin lucky, the lot of ya. If anything had happened to my daughter and I had survived, I would have come up here and threw each one of you off the fucking balcony. You little dickheads got away with one today. Next time, you might not be so lucky!" And out he stormed with his daughter, who was no older than six.

It dawned on me at that stage the gravity of my actions. Yes, we carried on smoking, drinking, and laughing afterwards, but I was genuinely scared for my life that day. I know I was not intending on hurting anyone when I posted fireworks through people's letter boxes; I was certainly not intending to hurt anyone with the TV, and even though I would sometimes carry a knife around, I never once intended to hurt anyone with it. But how messy all of those situations could have been for me as a child. In fact, I would go as far as to say, I was extremely lucky that all of those situations didn't end up much worse. And this is something I often talk to the young people about with my work with Elements.

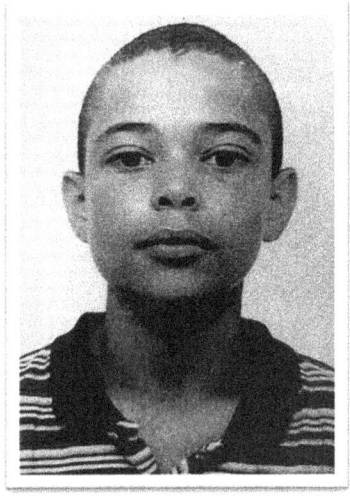

"Just because you don't intend on hurting anyone doesn't mean you won't."

We often succumb to dares and risky behaviour because of the fear of social repercussions; the term "pussy," for example, can trigger compliance out of a desire to avoid such labels. It takes a strong character to say, "call me a pussy all you want, but I ain't doing it." As a child I was very much a follower, and now all these experiences over time have turned me into the leader I am today.

Fifteen

Purpose

I strongly believe that each one of us serves a purpose. I serve a purpose and so do you. All our purposes are unique to us as individuals. The source of their beauty is our collective human ability to combine talents and build a better future for our children, demonstrating that shared purpose unites us.

It's a shame we live in a world of war, crime, famine, and poverty and hate crimes. It's a shame we live in a world full of envy, jealousy, rage, and trauma. However, these too serve a purpose within our world. They serve for us to learn and for us to prosper. More importantly, they serve a purpose for us to overcome, for us to understand that as a human species, we are so much better than war; we are so much better than famine and poverty.

We hold a shared responsibility as humans to unite and combat the true adversaries of our species: diseases, cancers, pathogens, climate issues, and all threats that endanger humanity.

It is imperative that we educate ourselves, striving to become better individuals. None of us enters this world flawless, nor will we depart from it without flaw. Thus, we must make the most of our abilities and knowledge, recognising that true value lies not in material wealth but in the connections, love, and wisdom we share with others.

It is our duty to contribute positively, regardless of our status, wealth, age, or background. This belief forms the core of my philosophy: every person has a unique purpose, akin to a gift waiting to be unwrapped. Discovering our individual roles and reasons for existence is a journey we all must embark on.

The feeling of being off course in life does not signify that you are not where you should be. Right now, in this very moment, you are exactly where you're supposed to be. So, then the question becomes, where do you want to be if you're not happy with where you are? You must be very clear about what that looks like and then once you've created that vision, that picture within your mind, you can create a plan for yourself so you can work each and every day to find your route to your own mountain top. Your next step is just in front of you. Take it, keep your head held high, and move forward with purpose and belief.

Sixteen

To Those Who Are Struggling

When life feels unbearable, when the loneliness cuts deep, and the weight of it all seems too heavy, know this you will get through it. The pain, the struggles, the lessons that seem impossible to make sense of right now, they're forging you into something stronger. Every trial is a step towards the next chapter, preparing you for the life you're meant to build.

Remember, if you take the easy road, your life may remain hard. But by choosing to face the hard things now, you'll pave a path to an easier, more fulfilling future. Don't fall into the trap of comparing your life to others. Your story is uniquely yours, with its own rhythm and purpose. Honour that. Celebrate that. Time is not your enemy it's your ally. The key is not how much time you have, but how you choose to use it. Focus on quality over quantity and dedicate yourself fully to the moments that matter.

Want more for yourself than anyone else could want for you. Be your biggest cheerleader, because not everyone will see your potential or understand your journey. And that's okay. What matters is that you believe in it.

Look after yourself not just your mind, but your body too. It's the vehicle that will carry you through this life, and the decisions you make today are shaping your tomorrow. There's a future version of you out there, smiling, thankful for the choices you had the courage to make now, even when it was hard.

Your struggle does not define you. Your resilience does. Keep pushing forward, even on the days that feel impossible, and watch as you rise—not because life got easier, but because you got stronger. You've got this.

To the Carer Who Never Stops Caring To the carer who pours their heart into the lives of young people,

even on days when the weight feels unbearable, this is for you. When you feel like the challenges are piling up, when you're questioning if you're really making a difference, take a moment and breathe. Because what you're doing matters more than words can say.

You see, they call them "hard to reach" kids, but perhaps they're not unreachable at all. They're just kids who've built walls to protect themselves, waiting for someone willing to climb over or carefully dismantle the bricks. And that's what you do, day in and day out. You find ways to reach beyond the surface, to touch hearts that have long been guarded. You're not just reaching them; you're teaching them what trust looks like, what compassion feels like, and what it means to be truly cared for.

Some days, the progress feels invisible, disguised under their silence or resistance. But remember, every kind word, every patient moment, every ounce of love you give is planting seeds. Seeds that may take time to grow, but trust me, they do grow. Years from now, those children will carry the echoes of your care as a compass guiding them through life.

It's okay to feel tired. It's okay to admit when you're struggling. Even the most selfless hearts need rest, and yours deserves it. But don't lose sight of this truth: you are their bridge, leading them from where they've been to where they could go. When the path seems steep, know that your resilience is their roadmap. When you feel unseen, know that their future success will make your impact visible in ways you could never have imagined.

You don't have to be perfect. Kids don't need perfection, they need presence. They need someone who shows up, even when it's hard. You become their proof that good people exist, that love doesn't always come with conditions, and that someone saw them as more than their mistakes, more than their pain.

It takes a special kind of strength to keep caring when the world feels heavy, and you have that strength. You're not just filling gaps in their lives; you're building foundations. You're proving that even in the face of struggles, love can shine through. And for that, you are a hero. Even on your hardest days, especially on your hardest days.

Keep going, because what you're doing changes lives not just theirs, but yours too. And when you look back one day, you'll see it. The progress, the smiles, the quiet moments that spoke louder than words. You'll see that it was all worth it.

Thank you for being someone who never stops caring, even when it's hard. You're not just reaching those kids; you're reaching into the future and shaping something brighter for them and for this world. Stay strong, because the hope you carry is the hope they need. You are seen, you are valued, and you are making a difference. Keep climbing. They're worth it, and so are you.

To Biddie My Birth Mother

Scan me

Seventeen

The Power of One

In 1995, when I was living in my first children's home, I asked Dave to be my dad. From that moment on, Dave has been the unwavering constant in my life. A source of support through every adventure, crisis, and celebration. For the past three decades, he has been my "Power of One," not only in those early days but throughout my entire journey.

Transforming Lives Through Consistent Care

In a world that often values collective action and systemic reform, we sometimes forget the quiet, transformative force of a single individual. Yet, for a child in care who may have experienced the disintegration of family, trust, and stability. Often the presence of just *one* consistent, caring adult that begins the healing process. This is the heart of the **power of one**.

The power of one is not a grand gesture or a sweeping reform. It's a gentle, steady commitment. It's the decision to listen without judgement, to advocate when it's hard, and to stay when it's easier to walk away. This determines whether a child survives or thrives within the care system.

The Personal Nature of Care

When children enter care, they often do so with layers of trauma, abandonment, or loss. Their understanding of adults is often shaped by inconsistency, mistrust, and instability. Policies provide a framework, but genuine transformation comes from connections.

One social worker who takes time to know a child beyond their file. One foster carer who stays committed despite difficult behaviour. One teacher who refuses to lower expectations. One advocate who ensures their voice is heard in meetings. Each of these individuals embodies the power of one. They create a sense of security and worth in children who may never have experienced such things before.

The Science of Connection

Strong attachment is important for emotional and mental wellbeing. For children in care, forming attachments is often difficult. They may fear rejection or believe they are unworthy of love. However, when just one adult remains available and consistent, something shifts.

Dr. Bruce Perry, leading psychologist, says healthy relationships aid trauma recovery, often starting with just one.

Nurturing relationships can lessen the impact of trauma over time because of the brain's ability to rewire itself. A child who has been hurt in a relationship can also be healed in a relationship. The power of one is not only emotional. It's a biological phenomenon. Love, attention, and presence change the brain.

The Role of Foster Carers

Foster carers are among the most visible and vital examples of the power of one. Even with other professionals involved, foster carers are often the constant presence in a child's life, from bedtime to school.

The Advocate's Voice

Beyond the home, children in care need professionals who will fight for their rights. A social worker who ensures a child's educational needs are met. A mentor who speaks up at a review. A judge who listens. The power of one also lies in *advocacy* using position and voice to protect and uplift a child's experience.

In the complex machinery of care, it's easy for children to feel invisible. Meetings can focus on risk, placement, and timelines. But when one professional insists, *"What does the child want?"* that simple question can change the direction of a case. It signals to the child that they are more than a number. That they matter.

The Long-Term Impact

When a child is believed in by one person, they are more likely to believe in themselves. They may still struggle, and the road may not be straight, but they envision a future.

Many adults who grew up in care reflect not on a whole system, but on an individual who stood out. "My key worker who always kept her word." "The foster dad who taught me how to ride a bike." "The teacher who said I was smart." These are the memories that shape resilience.

Even when young people leave care and face the challenges of independence, the impact of one trusted adult often echoes in their ability to persevere. It gives them an inner reference point of safety, care, and self-worth.

Why the Power of One Should Be Celebrated

In a world that often overlooks the quiet efforts of everyday heroes, we must **recognise and celebrate the power of one**. Not just as an abstract concept, but as a lived truth for countless children in care.

We celebrate the power of one because these individuals carry out acts of love, courage, and advocacy. Often without applause or recognition. Their impact is not always visible in the moment, but their presence often becomes a turning point in a child's life story.

These are the people who:

- Stay when it's hard
- Listen, when a child is silent
- Challenge systems when they're unjust
- Offer stability when the world feels unpredictable
- Believe in children before they believe in themselves

Celebrating the power of one reminds us that **ordinary people can do extraordinary things**. It shows how good, caring treatment is more important than system flaws.

It also nurtures **hope**, not just in children, but in carers and professionals who may feel invisible or exhausted. Recognition validates their efforts, renews their energy, and encourages others to rise to the same standard of care.

Celebrating the power of one says to the world: **"This child matters. And so does the person who stood by them."**

In doing so, we amplify a culture of kindness, resilience, and relational healing—one child, one adult, one connection at a time.

When the One is You

If you are a carer, social worker, teacher, youth worker, or mentor, you may not always see the impact of your presence. You may face resistance, burnout, or feel that nothing is changing. But the truth is this: *you may be the one*.

You may be the one who listens when others do not. You may be the one who stays when others have left. You may be the one who reflects love, value, and potential until the child believes it themselves.

You don't have to fix everything. You just have to be there, again and again.

A Collective of Ones

The power of one is multiplied when joined by like-minded people. We need better systems, policies that understand trauma, and more resources; but individuals must always be considered.

Because to a child in care, systems can feel distant. Change begins with someone who cares today.

Final Reflection

The power of one reminds us that genuine change doesn't always begin with institutions, campaigns, or funding. It begins with a person. One person. Who cares, acts consistently, and believes in a child when no one else does.

For children in care, this is not a cliché. It's a lifeline.

May we all recognise the power we hold to influence one life, and may we never underestimate how much that matters.

Drip By Drip Day By Day

Drip By Drip Day By Day

Steven Russell

Eighteen

Letters to Steven

Dear Steven

I Love You

I was born in November 1964, in Kitts Green Birmingham, to Irish parents. I gave birth to you, Steven, in 1985, a moment that filled my world with light and purpose. But when your father passed away just months later, in November 1985, my life began to unravel. The devastation left me broken, and I fell into the depths of despair, enduring multiple stays at Hollymoor Psychiatric Hospital in Birmingham. Yet through it all, my love for you remained unwavering, it gave me strength when I thought I had none left.

Steven, I fought for you. I fought to keep you close, through endless court battles and sleepless nights filled with tears. In one case, I even stopped social services from adopting you away from me the judge himself said I was a good mother. I held on to every precious moment we shared, like seeing you on your birthdays and at Christmas. I brought you gifts, like the police uniform and the clown and I made sure you had school uniforms. Every visit to Pat's left me aching inside. I didn't show you my heartbreak, but after I left, I cried for hours, wishing things could be different.

You remind me so much of your father. His clean-cut style, his height, even the way you wear your goatee as an adult—it's like seeing him again. You are smart, kind, and strong, Steven, and you carry the best of both of us. I hope you know how much I loved you then and how fiercely I love you now.

Life has been cruel to me in many ways. Since the stroke in 2018, the physical toll has left me paralyzed, my hair gone, and my spirit dimmed. I chose not to let the grandkids see me like this because I wanted to protect them from the image of my frailty. But with every passing day, the absence burns inside me. Steven, I love you and your children more than words can express, even if you don't love me back. Sometimes, you can just feel it when someone doesn't love you, and the ache of that realisation is unbearable.

Still, I hold onto the memories the joy, the laughter, the moments when you were mine. Steven, you are my heart, my pride, and my enduring love. I wish you and your beautiful family all the happiness in the world. May life bring you everything good and bright, even if I can no longer be part of it.

Forever yours,
Biddy
(Biological Mum)

Dear Steven,

I hope this letter finds you in a place of peace and comfort. As I sit down to write to you, I am overwhelmed by memories of the time we spent together and the bond we shared, a bond that remains close to my heart despite the many years and miles that may separate us now.

I remember the first day you came into my life, a bright-eyed and curious little boy who quickly found his way into our hearts. My daughters adored you, and it didn't take long for you to become a cherished member of our family. You brought so much joy and laughter into our home, Steven, and for that, I will always be grateful.

Life was not always easy for you, I know. Losing your father at such a tender age and navigating the complexities of foster care must have felt like an uphill battle at times. But even through the challenges, you displayed a resilience and strength that inspired us all. You had your moments of stubbornness, your fiery determination, but those qualities made you uniquely you. Your love for adventure, your mischievous grin, and the way you lit up every room you entered—these are memories I hold close.

I remember how my sister's husband, who was from the Caribbean, with his warm and cheerful nature, would spend time with you. He would kick a football around with you in the garden and tinker in the shed, always patient and kind. Those little moments of connection seemed to light up your face, and it reminded me of how much love you truly deserved.

I often think about the trips we took together, the days spent at Weston-Super-Mare in the caravan, and our explorations of Cheddar Gorge. Those were magical times, Steven, filled with laughter, bonding, and the simple joys of family. You were always so eager to explore the world and take in its beauty, and those moments remind me of the vibrant spirit you possess.

When you moved on to your "Forever family," I had hoped and prayed it would bring you stability and happiness, though my heart ached at the thought of you leaving us. I trusted the decisions made by the social services team, believing they had your best interests at heart. I never imagined you might endure anything less than love and care. Knowing now that you faced struggles and hurt in that home, I am deeply saddened and wish I could have done more to protect you.

I remember how your mother would visit, her attempts at connection often falling short in your eyes. She was a stranger to you, and I saw the frustration and confusion in your heart. When she issued threats to me, it hurt deeply but my concern was always for you, Steven. You deserved love, stability, and understanding, and I tried my best to provide that for you during our time together.

You were a gorgeous child, Steven inside and out. Yes, you could be argumentative, and you struggled at school, but those were small facets of a much larger, beautiful picture. You were kind, full of potential, and had an incredible spirit that shone brightly even in the darkest moments. Watching you grow was a privilege, and I cherished every moment, even the challenging ones.

When I learned of your placement in a children's home, my heart broke. I wanted so desperately to bring you back into our family, to give you the love and stability you so deserved. I hope that wherever you are now, you know just how much you mean to me and how deeply I care for you.

Steven, you have always been and will always be special to me. You are strong, resilient, and deserving of every happiness life can offer. I hope this letter reminds you of the love that surrounded you, not just in my home, but in the hearts of everyone who truly saw the incredible person you are.

Please know that you are always in my thoughts and prayers. If you ever need a listening ear, advice, or even just someone to reminisce with, I am here. You will always have a place in my heart and my life.

With endless love and care,

Pat

Dear Steven,

When I first met you, Steven, you were a nervous little soul. You seemed so small for your age, lonely and frightened. Your hands would tremble constantly, and it broke my heart to see the weight you carried. To me, you felt like a lost soul in need of someone to care, someone to truly see you. I knew, in that moment, I had to be there for you.

You brought life into every room with your cheeky smile and quick wit, demanding attention in the way only you could. Others may have seen you as difficult, selfish, or even angry, but I saw so much more. I saw a young man who needed stability after the chaos of being moved around so much. I made a choice, Steven, to treat you with kindness and love, to meet you where you were, even when it meant stepping away from what the rules dictated. Because I couldn't bear to see another young person, like you, fall into despair.

I will never forget the night you asked me if I would be your dad. We were at Sutton Road Children's Home, and your words floored me. They carried so much weight, so much longing. It made me sad for the boy you were and the love I knew you'd been searching for.

Years passed, and when I bumped into you on the street, I saw the man you were becoming. You spoke of the life you were leading one filled with choices I worried about, like smoking cannabis and other things I didn't even want to imagine. But I admired your resilience, your determination to turn things around when you were ready. And you did, Steven. You set goals for yourself and achieved them in ways that left me so proud.

I'll never forget teaching you to drive. Those early days were a bit rocky literally, with a couple of crashes but you stuck with it and became a skilled driver. True to yourself, you even picked out a car with style, complete with blacked-out windows. You always had a flair for individuality.

There were moments when I tried to guide you in other ways too, like when I saw you getting caught up in casual relationships. I wanted you to respect yourself more, to see your own worth. Even when you didn't fully take my advice at first, I know now that you listened. Over time, you started to make choices that reflected the respect you deserved.

The day you told me that you and Laura were expecting a baby is still fresh in my mind. You were so upset, scared even, feeling unprepared for fatherhood. But I saw it as a turning point for you, and I told you so. I reassured you that this child could become your greatest reason to grow, and that you were more ready than you realised. And you proved me right, Steven.

To this day, you and I remain close. I know your children well, and I am so honoured to treat them all as my Godchildren, even if only one is officially so. Watching you become the man, the father, that you are today fills me with so much pride and joy.

Steven, I'm so grateful that I was able to be there for you when you needed someone the most. You were lost, but you found your way. And in doing so, you've enriched my life beyond words.

With love and pride,

Dave

Dear Steven,

From the very first moment we met you, we knew you were special. We remember visiting you at the children's home, sitting together and talking, learning about your world, and watching the way your eyes lit up when you spoke about wanting to be part of a family. And when the day came for your first overnight stay, we saw your excitement, the way you packed your things, ready to step into a new chapter. We were just as ready as you.

There were challenges, of course. School wasn't always easy, and settling in took time. But through it all, you persevered. You learned, grew, and found your way, proving time and again just how strong and determined you are.

You were never one to sit still, never one to simply wait for life to happen you always chased after it. Whether it was selling insurance, working in the factory, or finding your own place, you kept moving forward, never letting anything hold you back. We saved money for you until you found your footing, and then you met Dave, then Laura and just like that, you spread your wings.

Steven, you have always been observant, always watching to see who truly cared and we hope you always knew that we did, with everything in us. We stood by you, encouraged you to build a strong relationship with your, reminded you that forgiveness could heal, and gave you our home, our love, and our family. You adapted so quickly, embraced our ways, learned about skin care, saving, and looking after your clothes. And goodness, how well you dressed always with style, always looking your best.

You were never afraid to work hard, never afraid to go after what you wanted. Even when you were between jobs, you kept searching, kept striving, because you knew how much it mattered. You helped with our catering business, played football with the boys, ran across the park and climbed trees, built friendships, and became part of something bigger than yourself. And oh, how you loved the church, singing, praying, always giving thanks to the Lord. You left a mark on everyone, and even now, people ask for you, remembering your warmth, your kindness, your spirit.

Steven, we are so proud of you. We have watched you grow, watched you find your way, watched you become a man who is strong, loving, and caring. You deserve everything good that life has to offer, and we will always be cheering for you, always holding space for you in our hearts.

With all our love,
Eunice & Neville

Nineteen

Dear Steven

Dear Steven,

I know your trust in the adults around you has disappeared, just as they seem to vanish every time you start building a new relationship. Countless unanswered questions and empty spaces linger, ones that even your future self cannot fill because, at this moment, you are living it, experiencing the hurt and the pain. You often ask yourself, "Where do I belong?" and "Do I belong anywhere?" I understand the sting you feel when you see other children returning to school after Christmas, their faces alight with stories about the fun they had with their families and the expensive gifts they received. It feels as though you're not good enough for those conversations, that you're distant from a place where you long to belong, a place where you are seen. To be noticed, you behave in ways that ensure you're seen. It's easy to make others laugh when you feel so sad inside.

What you can't see yet, Steven, is that all these experiences are teaching you to understand different people and developing your empathy. Empathy is the ability to feel what others feel.

This is why, when the children cry, you instinctively reach out to them, and when they laugh, you laugh too. You share their emotional experiences, making them feel seen, supporting them in sadness, and sharing joy in happiness. You have spent so much time trying to make others smile, sometimes you forget to smile yourself. I know you sprayed the windows with your water gun, making Pat laugh by pretending it's raining because you didn't want to stay outside.

I know you threw pebbles onto the neighbour's grass as he was mowing the lawn to get his attention because he couldn't hear your requests for your blow-up hammer. And I know about the drawing pin you placed under Mrs Summers' chair out of frustration. When you go on the school trip to Sherwood Forest to learn about Robin Hood, I have a challenge for you: don't draw on Ashley's arm with your new pen. He laughed at you for not having a bow and arrow, but drawing on him will only show him you're the same. You are a good friend, Steven, even when others don't realise it yet.

I know how hard it is to be surrounded by children who have what you've always wanted. A family, but not just any family, your own. There's a voice inside that tells you that you don't belong in a family because you're naughty and who wants to take care of a bad kid? That's your pain voice talking, Steven, created by all the hurt you've faced in such a short time. Pat, she gets you. She protects, educates, and loves you. It wasn't her choice for you to leave; it was out of her control. Brave you were for the time you lived with the *"Forever family."* Every day reminded you that you weren't part of their family. As an adult, you'll read your care records and see it was your behaviour that was blamed. But you and I know the truth, don't we? Let's uncover it.

Naturally, you struggled with the maternal figure, the supposed mother. With Pat, it was natural because you grew up seeing her as a mother, though she wasn't your biological one. But your new mummy was also named Pat, which complicated things. I know you weren't lazy when you wet the bed; you had a condition called Nocturnal Enuresis. It must have been embarrassing to be told you were lazy by your new family when you needed support and understanding. You faced a cruel choice, hide the sheets or tell your new parents, knowing their response would be blame and shame. You chose the safer path, even if it wasn't the right one.

"Hold your breath, Steven, I'm right here with you". Having your head held underwater is a cruelty no child should endure, yet you did, all because of hair-washing. You realised then that this wasn't your forever family. When given a choice between a hanger or a wooden spoon, the wooden spoon seemed to hurt less. You planned to run away with Ashton from school, even mapped it out, but never went through with it. "Go to bed." I don't know how much time you spent there, but it felt like a lifetime. "Is Steven coming out to play?"

"No, he's been naughty." Those words echoed on hot summer days when friends called for you.

In the future, children will spend most of their time on screens, no, not TV's but mobile phones that will become an unhealthy magnet for kids, interacting through messages rather than face-to-face play. You were part of the lucky generation that didn't have screens, though you spent so much time alone. This theme of solitude runs through your life, which is why you created an imaginary friend named John. Without a consistent adult presence, you needed something permanent, and John became your best friend. He became your forever family. Carers will ask who you are talking to as you have these conversations. John was warmth and safety, never letting you down. He was a loving presence, even feeling spiritual, reminding you every day that you would be okay.

Hold on, Steven. Hold on. This pain will transform you into something special.

I see you, Steven. I see you crying yourself to sleep in new homes, hiding at school with your arms tucked in your coat, finding comfort in a toy from a McDonald's Happy Meal. I see you falling out of a tree, landing in stinging nettles, feeling the physical and emotional pain from apathetic parents. I see you being left at home while others went to see the new Free Willy movie, punished for being 'naughty.' I see you pulled into your foster sister's room, experiencing something incomprehensible, something you couldn't talk about. I see you getting sick after trying cigarettes in your second children's home, becoming addicted. I see you moving from school to school, struggling academically, blamed for your behaviours and lack of concentration. And I see you at 19, bloodied in a street fight in Birmingham. I know why you created an invisible friend, why you talked to toys, why you sought comfort in Blue Bear. I know why you hide and shout, why you push people away.

What you need is connection and stability. That's where Dave enters your life. He makes you laugh, plays games with you, reads bedtime stories, and takes you camping. He plants a small seed of hope in your heart, showing you that not all adults are unsafe. Little do you know, Steven, but Dave will rejoin your path at 16. Until then, life has more lessons for you.

When Pat discovers you are in Sutton Road Children's Home, she wants you back. You write a letter to the judge, explaining why you should return to Pat, and you do. Despite changing schools and leaving friends, you're willing to return to the mother who loved you from the start. The pain stored over three years began to surface like a volcano, and you didn't know how to manage it.

You became too difficult for Pat to support, but it wasn't her fault, nor yours. Emotional resilience work was never done, leaving you to manage emotions alone, blamed when wrong. Today, we call it emotional regulation, with adults focusing on building safe, non-judgmental relationships. Some schools and homes still don't understand, but as an adult, you're working on it. One day, you'll be the boss of your own children's support service, called Elements. Everything works out for you in the end, Steven. You just have to go through this to become who you're meant to be.

Conversations about mum are sticky. I know you don't see her as your mum, the closest was Pat, but you were taken from her. Your emotions toward your mum mix anger, confusion, and hurt. She's a stranger, hence calling her 'biddy.' Your mum herself had a tough life, growing up in care, facing abuse, losing a child to adoption. She fought to get you back after your dad passed, despite battles. Every chance she gets, she sees you, never missing a birthday or Christmas. Your mum is a fighter, Steven, and you inherit this spirit. In another life, maybe you'd have an amazing mother-son relationship, but these are the cards we're dealt.

One day, you'll make a tribute video for her to let go of the past.

Each day is a step towards your purpose. Some things in life are learned, others you're born with. You were born to heal, given your experiences and the impact you'll have on many lives. You have an energetic spark that lights up a room, a gift of happiness, joy, and love. Master this gift, or the dark side rage, anger, resentment will take over. Focus on the purpose, let it drown out the darkness. Your energy is warm and inviting, allowing others to be near you. You connect with people, ensuring fairness and understanding. As you grow, you'll follow others who don't have your best interests at heart, but this is an important lesson. You'll understand what feels right and wrong as you transition into adulthood. Disruptions and interruptions have marred your lifelong search for meaning, purpose, and connection. You'll search for meaning in places that break you down, only to carve you into the person who inspires young people like yourself. Be that person for them, where they lacked one until they met you.

The easy part of writing to you is that you don't need to change anything. Keep listening to that inner voice whether it's John or guidance because it's leading you where you need to be. Your journey has been difficult, and challenges emotionally and physically painful. This pain is akin to ink in your pen of life, writing your story, your pain-to-purpose story. Only you can tell this story, only you will understand what it takes to make it. This isn't a cliché about better days or an inspiring talk for lonely nights. It's a message only you can deliver to yourself.

So, this is it, Steven. Let the world see your infectious cheeky smile and hear that silly giggle. Let adversity and pain be the fuel for your better future. For when we are born, we don't get to choose the cards we are dealt. But we get to choose how we play them and just because you can't stop the waves, doesn't mean you won't learn to surf.

Drip by Drip, Day by Day, it isn't easy, but you'll find a way!

Steven, words can't describe how proud you make me feel. Your journey is a testament to your incredible strength and resilience. You have turned every challenge into an opportunity for growth. Your story is one of hope and inspiration for the future generations you will go onto inspire.

All the love in the world,

From your best friend and biggest supporter,

Big Steven

Oh, I almost forgot to mention, in Year 8, you'll be appearing on CITV playing the steel drums for their 1998 Christmas show. The onset director will ask you to remove the tinsel from your hair before filming. While I already know the answer, can you guess what you'll do lol? (lol means laugh out loud)

Big Love little man x

P.S.. and when you are almost 40 you take a trip to Barbados, where you find home, peace and family.

Drip By Drip Day By Day

About the Author

Steven Russell brings a powerful and unique voice to his memoir, ***Drip by Drip, Day by Day: Finding Purpose Through the Pain.*** Growing up in the care system in Birmingham, UK, Steven's early life was marked by challenges that ignited a deep passion for championing children and young people. For over two decades, he has dedicated his career to empowering others, working across social care and education sectors to lift hundreds of lives.

A proud father of three, Malachi, Cory, and Alyssa, Steven is the founding director of Element Support CIC and Elements Educational Training Limited. These organisations are committed to nurturing the social and emotional well-being of children, young people, and the practitioners who support them, offering tools and strategies that strengthen connections and build resilience.

With his memoir, Steven seeks to inspire those who share the care experience, giving voice to the little boy he once was and shedding light on the endurance and courage it takes to overcome life's trials. His story is a call to others to find purpose through pain, to rise above and overcome adversity, and to believe in the possibility of a brighter future.

Steven's unwavering optimism shines through in his belief that life chances for children and young people can change for the better. Not because of systems, but because of the extraordinary people working within them, making all the difference. His work and words are a testament to hope, fortitude, and the power of connection.

Connect with Steven Russell
Website: www.dual-perspective.co.uk
Email: steven@dual-perspective.co.uk

www.marciampublishinghouse.com

www.ingramcontent.com/pod-product-compliance
Lightning Source LLC
Chambersburg PA
CBHW040245010526
44119CB00057B/820